THE THEOLOGY OF
THE PASSION OF THE CHRIST

Monica Migliorino Miller draws on a wide range of published critical comment to present an apologia for Mel Gibson's film on the Passion, at the same time skillfully refreshing one's memory of the film. Into this, with theological competence and spiritual insight, she weaves reflection on the significance of the sacrifice of Christ for the human story.

Francis Cardinal George, OMI
Archbishop of Chicago

For the many devout Christians who were deeply moved by the film *The Passion of the Christ*, Dr. Monica Miller's book will be an excellent guide to discussion. Her work is filled with serious questions, answers, and details about the film and its relationship to the traditional Christian theology on the sufferings and death of Our Lord. If you were touched by the film, you will find this book enlightening and a source of much meditation.

Father Benedict J. Groeschel, CFR

With critical as well as theological insight, Monica Miller cuts through the confusions behind much of the controversy over *The Passion*, from fastidious objections to its emphasis on blood and suffering to misguided complaints about its lack of concern with ordinary dramatic notions of character development and plot structure. Miller decisively refutes the critics who failed to see the religious meaning of Gibson's film, and opens new worlds of meaning for appreciative viewers wishing to enter more deeply into *The Passion*'s mysteries.

Steven D. Greydanus
Film critic, *National Catholic Register*
& DecentFilms.com

Visit our web site at
www.albahouse.org
(for orders www.alba-house.com)
or call 1-800-343-2522 (ALBA)
and request current catalog

The Theology of
THE PASSION OF
THE CHRIST

Monica Migliorino Miller

ST PAULS

Alba
House

Library of Congress Cataloging-in-Publication Data

Miller, Monica Migliorino, 1953-.
   The theology of The passion of the Christ / Monica Migliorino Miller.
      p. cm.
   ISBN 0-8189-0975-7
1. Passion of the Christ (Motion picture)   I. Title.

   PN1997.2.P39M55 2005
   791.43'72—dc22
                              2004024667

Produced and designed in the United States of America by the
Fathers and Brothers of the Society of St. Paul,
2187 Victory Boulevard, Staten Island, New York 10314-6603,
as part of their communications apostolate.

ISBN: 0-8189-0975-7

Printing Information:

Current Printing - first digit   3   4   5   0   7   0   0   10

Year of Current Printing - first year shown

2006   2007   2008   2009   2010   2011   2012   2013

For our Treasures,
Bernadette, Joseph and Patrick

Acknowledgments

The author would like to thank several individuals with whom she had conversation and in-depth discussions about Mel Gibson's film, *The Passion of the Christ*—conversations that eventually sparked the idea that a book on the theology of this very unique movie was much needed. I especially thank Professor Janet Smith of Sacred Heart Seminary of the Archdiocese of Detroit for her expertise, insight and encouragement for this project. I also thank Professor Martin Brenner of SS. Cyril and Methodius Seminary, Fr. William Thomas and Robert Christian of Holy Spirit Parish in Hamburg, Michigan; David and Kathleen Moss of the Association of Hebrew Catholics, Russell and John Hittenger, Tim and Kathy Herrman, Dr. Thomas Woods, Dr. Barbara Laboissonniere, Jan LaFave, Laura Nelson, Samy and Alica Wong, Dan and Linda Kelly, and Suzanne Housey. I would like to thank my students at St. Mary's College of Madonna University: Kristina Younan, Steve Pullis, Robert Klesko, Maria Valens and Ben Beckett.

I am especially grateful to my assistant at St. Mary's College, Allan Koluch, for his diligent research and for reading the manuscript. He was a true help to me in the writing of this book. I also thank John G. Powers for reading the manuscript and making many helpful corrections.

A special note of thanks is given to Fr. Donald Keefe, S.J., my professor at Marquette University. I will always be indebted to the genius of his theological insight.

Special thanks to Barbara R. Nicolosi for providing the Preface to this book.

Finally, thank you Edmund, my dear husband, for your love, support and encouragement.

Monica Migliorino Miller, PhD

Table of Contents

The Passion of the Christ
Film Credits

Crew:

Director:	Mel Gibson
Screenplay:	Benedict Fitzgerald and Mel Gibson
Producers:	Bruce Davey, Mel Gibson, and Stephen McEveety
Director of Photography:	Caleb Deschanel
Composer:	John Debney
Production Designer:	Francesco Frigeri
Set Decorator:	Carlo Gervasi
Editor:	John Wright
Special Effects Makeup:	Keith Vanderlaan and Greg Cannom
Costume Designer:	Maurizio Millenotti

Cast:

James Caviezel	*Jesus*
Monica Bellucci	*Magdalene*
Claudia Gerini	*Claudia Procles*
Maia Morgenstern	*Mary*
Hristo Naumov	*Pontius Pilate*
Sergio Rubini (I)	*Dismas*
Mattia Sbragia	*Caiaphas*
Toni Bertorelli	*Annas*
Roberto Bestazzoni	*Malchus*
Francesco Cabras	*Gesmas*
Giovanni Capalbo	*Cassius*
Rosalinda Celentano	*Satan*
Emilio De Marchi (I)	*Scornful Roman*
Francesco De Vito	*Peter*
Lello Giulivo	*Brutish Roman*
Abel Jefry	*Second Temple Officer*
Hristo Jivkov	*John*

Preface

In his 1999 *Letter to Artists*, Pope John Paul II reminded us all that beyond being just the product of theological reflection, sacred art is, itself, actually a source of theology. The artist who seriously pursues what the Pope calls "epiphanies of beauty" becomes a vehicle of revelation between God and His people. So, for example, any study of Eucharist would be incomplete without time spent absorbing the cadences of the 17th century hymn, *Let All Mortal Flesh Keep Silent*, or the benediction poem, *Tantum Ergo*, written by St. Thomas Aquinas.

Who in the Church at the end of the 20th century, would have imagined that within a few years, the most significant 'source of theology' about the passion and death of Jesus Christ, would come out of Hollywood? In seeking to create what he has called "the Stations of the Cross in my art form,"* filmmaker Mel Gibson has planted the image of the Cross back in the consciousness of the Church with the compelling power of cinema.

The sacred artist's task, as an instrument of Divine Grace, is to bring forth something beautiful. In this case, Mel Gibson achieved this task in a stunning way. His project was accompanied by the requisite sacrifices that render our human offerings holy—in Gibson's case, financial risk and public opprobrium. In a ten year creative process, Gibson brought forth the most sig-

---

* Words of Mel Gibson as he accepted the Catholics in Media Award for *The Passion of the Christ*, November 7, 2004 at the Beverly Hills Hilton.

nificant piece of religious cinema ever made. It is beyond Mel Gibson's task, as sacred artist, to also have to intuit all the theological meanings underlying the work of his hands. This is why we need theologians.

I experienced this as regards this project in June of 2003, when I had the privilege to attend a private screening of the rough-cut of *The Passion of the Christ* with Mel Gibson. There was also a Protestant Biblical scholar at the screening, and afterward, he kept pressing Gibson to explain the exact significance of the "ugly baby" who appears during the scourging sequence. Gibson tried a few sentences to get at what he was attempting through the image, and then, finally shrugged. "I wanted something *really* creepy in that moment. Didn't you think it was creepy?" Yes, all of Christendom, and even the pagan world beyond has experienced that moment of cinematic creepiness. Creating it was the job of the artist. Explaining why the image affected us all so strongly is the job of the theologian.

But there is a much more basic question for our theologians and ecclesial historians that arises out of the astounding global success of *The Passion of the Christ*. Why this story, told this way in this moment?

In terms of cinematic storytelling and style, *The Passion of the Christ* seemed to come out of nowhere. One would have to look back to the hey-day of silent cinema to find artistic antecedents for Gibson's use of visual imagery. In a similar way, the film had no thematic antecedents, at least in post-Conciliar Christendom. We just weren't talking about the sufferings of the Messiah that much in the Church before February of 2004, and certainly not with the brutal intensity of Gibson's devout lens. We were all going about our business, as Christ says in the Gospels, eating and drinking and carrying on, and then, *The Passion of the Christ* took us all by surprise. And then led millions and millions of us to our knees in heartfelt compunction. I remember leaving a rough-cut screening of the film in June of 2003, and praying over and over in my car, "Jesus, I'm so sorry. I forgot." Why did the faithful flock to this film, and why did it work so profoundly with so many of us?

Monica Miller has done an important service to the People of God, by considering *The Passion of the Christ* as a source of theology. Pushing beyond the political, social and even ecclesial controversies that must always accompany the Cross as the Sign of Contradiction, her book asks us all to reverentially regard the film, and allow it to deepen our understanding of the mystery of Calvary. It is a humble task for a Catholic theologian to be led by the ruminations of a contemporary artist—and, how much more one from Hollywood?!—but, in so doing, Miller sets an example of exactly what the Pope means in calling for "a renewal of the fruitful dialogue" between the Church and the arts.

In unraveling the meaning of the separate parts of the film, Dr. Miller reveals the answer to the broad question as to the film's power with the People of God today. Contrary to some of the charges by some theologians, *The Passion of the Christ* is not a throwback to the Church of another time. It connects the Church of today with the cries of the People of God that have ascended through the ages. For we too, in the 21st century are a people who need saving and the *sensus fideii* belongs to us as to the Church in any other generation. In affirming the theology that underlies the project, Dr. Miller has listened to the voice of the artist, and to the voices of the sheep. Her work goes a long way to demonstrating that *The Passion of the Christ* "worked" with believers for one reason: it brought them into encounter with their Shepherd, in His most compelling posture as the Lamb of God.

Barbara R. Nicolosi

Film As Ritual

THE PASSION OF THE CHRIST is not simply a movie—it is a religious experience. As it is the fruit of Mel Gibson's personal faith commitment and piety, the movie at least intends to create a religious experience. Like the New Testament Scriptures, upon which it takes its structure, form, and content, this film's author, and even the actor who plays the movie's central role, intend for *The Passion* to be a religious expression. And, like the Bible and the Christian faith, *The Passion* is not neutral. This movie is a work of art with a committed point of view—the sort of commitment that one can expect from people who take their religious faith seriously.

Since the invention of motion pictures in the early 20th century the life of Christ has seen dozens of film interpretations— some faithful to the Gospels, some not. Hollywood epics such as 1961's *King of Kings* and 1965's *The Greatest Story Ever Told*, while cinematically flawed, are very respectful, pietistic, and express a kind of awe of the Christian faith. *The Passion of the Christ* is not about awe or respect. Like its celluloid predecessors, it contains its measure of these elements. But it truly can be said that *The Passion of the Christ*, as a movie about Jesus, is in a category all its own.

The ultimate reason for the difference is that the man who put this story to film is a committed Christian—moreover a committed Christian in the Catholic tradition. *The Passion* represents Gibson's Christian faith as it is rooted in Scripture and (because he is a Catholic) in Sacred Tradition.

It should not disturb the viewer of *The Passion* that this is Gibson's movie. Simply because it is his vision of the faith does not at all mean that *The Passion* is therefore a narrow and private expression. The movie cannot be so easily dismissed, just as the great works of Michelangelo or Rembrandt cannot be dismissed even though their artistic expression is unique to them. Regardless of their own personal faith, such artists of the past brought to life in stone and canvas not simply their own points of view, but the universal Christian faith of the Church. In short, such artists remained faithful to the Christian message that is handed on from one generation to the next. Gibson's movie is within this great artistic tradition. Indeed, even Hollywood movies about Jesus have appeal because, despite being made by people who do not necessarily profess Christianity, they stick to the Gospels *as Christianity understands those Gospels*—i.e., Jesus is the divine Son of God, Jesus' death is redemptive, Jesus rose from the dead, etc., etc.

Perhaps for the first time in movie history four things came together to make *The Passion* the unique film that it is. First, the director of the movie is a person of deep Christian faith. Second, he intended his film to be an expression of that faith. Third, he funded the project with his own money, thus achieving control over the product. Fourth, he had the talent of artistic expression to successfully bring his religious vision to film.

When I say that *The Passion* functions as a religious experience, this is certainly not to say that it will be a religious experience for all those who see it. Many people who profess the Christian faith have not found the movie religiously affirming or inspiring for a variety of reasons. Many non-Christians find the movie repulsive. For some it is too violent. Others reject it because *The Passion* is, ironically, too biblical for them. One reviewer commented that the movie was "the cinematic equivalent of a Rorschach inkblot: You will probably see in it whatever you choose to see in it."[1] This is not to say that Gibson intends for the viewer to see whatever he or she wishes, but like a Rorschach, one will see according to what one brings to the film, and not only on a political, intellectual, artistic, emotional, or psychological level. Reactions to the movie really depend upon one's own spirituality. As one commentator stated, "Gibson's film places the bulk of the responsibility on the viewer."[2] The movie will affect people according to their knowledge of and commitment to Christ or their willingness to be moved by the Christian story.

Why Just The Passion?

Many critics fault *The Passion* for "its presumption that an audience unfamiliar with the horrific sacrifice Christ made will know what led him to the cross, will understand how his teaching deviated from that of the Jewish leaders and will appreciate how radical his message of love, forgiveness and redemption seemed to be."[3] The film, of course, has several flashbacks that show Jesus preaching, at home with Mary, forgiving Mary Magdalen, and teaching His apostles. But even the flashbacks serve as theological commentary on the central action of the film, namely the sacrifice of Christ. They do not provide any substantial biographical or historical context. There is very limited character development in the film and no real plot development. Many who have viewed the film question if it is a good piece of film making. Roger Ebert, veteran film critic for the *Chicago Sun-Times*, asked:

---

[1] James Sanford, "The Passion of the Christ," *Kalamazoo Gazette*, February 2004.
[2] Russell Hittinger and Elizabeth Lev, "Gibson's *Passion*," *First Things*, March 2004.
[3] Terry Lawson, "Gibson's Vision is One of Beauty and Violence," *Detroit Free Press*, February 25, 2004.

Is the film "good" or "great"? I imagine each person's reaction (visceral, theological, artistic) will differ. I was moved by the depth of feeling, by the skill of the actors and technicians, by their desire to see this project through no matter what. To discuss individual performances, such as Jim Caviezel's heroic depiction of the ordeal, is almost beside the point. This isn't a movie about performances, although it has powerful ones, or about technique, although it is awesome, or about cinematography (although Caleb Deschanel paints with an artist's eye) or music (although John Debney supports the content without distracting from it).

It is a film about an idea. An idea that it is necessary to fully comprehend the Passion if Christianity is to make any sense. Gibson has communicated his idea with a single-minded urgency. Many will disagree. Some will agree, but be horrified by the graphic treatment. I myself am no longer religious in the sense that a long-ago altar boy thought he should be, but I can respond to the power of belief whether I agree or not, and when I find it in a film, I must respect it.[4]

The Passion is a religious meditation—celluloid is simply the medium. Instead of reading a poem, a holy book of prayers, the life of a saint, listening to sacred music, or looking at an icon or religious painting, Gibson, who is by trade a film-maker, has made a religious movie. When compared to a theatrical work it bears closest resemblance to the "passion play"—staged dramatizations, whether by professional theater companies or local church groups, of the last twelve hours of Christ's life. Such dramatizations date back over a thousand years. The most famous

---

[4] Roger Ebert, "The Passion of the Christ," *Chicago Sun-Times*, February 24, 2004.

is the passion play of the German town of Oberammergau. Since 1634 the village residents have staged a passion play every ten years in fulfillment of a vow to God for having spared their town during an outbreak of the bubonic plague that killed 15,000 residents in Munich.

Gibson's *Passion* is not simply a pious dramatization of the suffering of Christ. The movie functions as an icon. As any icon, it not only visually communicates religious truths, but also intends to draw the viewer into those truths. It intends to stimulate, arouse and provoke faith or—if not genuine faith—then at least some kind of response to the person of Christ and His mission of redemption.

> [Gibson] is not just telling another Bible tale. He's preaching—and his decision to use provocative, even jarring modernist techniques implies that it is not a polite sermon that would please upper-middle-class, American, suburban Protestants. It's blunt, aggressive, even confrontational—a working class Roman Catholic or hell-fire-and-damnation Baptist approach. Visually Gibson employs street-preacher tactics, refusing to let a potential audience member get away, but instead following him down the block and peppering him with increasingly provocative rhetorical questions until he gets a reaction. He's doing whatever he has to do to make this story personal.[5]

The Passion has little or no character or plot development for a reason. It functions like a Christian religious painting. When someone goes to a museum, strolls through the galleries and comes across a painting that depicts a man filled with wounds hanging on a cross with a veiled woman weeping on one side

---

[5] Matt Zoller Seitz, "Red-State Deicide," *New York Press*, February 26, 2004.

and a young man praying on the other, no one faults the painting because it lacks historical background information. Only those who know the Christian religion will understand the painting. Only those who know the Christian religion will be able to supply the necessary spiritual context by which the painting can be ultimately appreciated. Gibson's *Passion* functions on this level. Like a painting that graphically depicts the sufferings of Christ, the viewer is immediately confronted and may feel quite unsettled and disturbed by such terrible inhumanity. If one does not know the Christian story, the full meaning of the artistic display of this inhumanity will be lost on the viewer.[6] Any religious painting that depicts the life of Christ, if it is a good painting, will provide the viewer with insight into his or her faith, but the viewer must possess some level of faith, or at least knowledge of the faith, to understand the work of art. It is obvious that Gibson is not much interested in just providing a good dramatization of the life of Christ. For that Franco Zeffirelli's well-rendered *Jesus of Nazareth* will do very nicely, but while the "beautiful faces and rich settings have a tapestry-like quality… we never quite forget that we are watching a 371-minute-long visual ornamentation of a textural narrative. For religious people, and probably for most viewers it is perfectly safe viewing… it is not a work of art that haunts the viewer."[7]

It can be argued that Gibson could have made a better movie had he spent more time informing the audience about who Jesus is and the nature of His mission. After all, this is a movie shown in thousands of theaters that cater to a wide and diverse audience. It is not a religious painting meant to adorn a church. But this is exactly why *The Passion* is a phenomenon. A religious faith statement managed to burst into the center of secularized culture and—if one can judge from the box office returns—it

---

6 For a good discussion of this issue see Steve Greydanus, "Understanding the Catholic Meaning of The Passion of the Christ," www.decentfilms.com

7 Hittinger and Lev.

was a hugely successful intrusion. Nonetheless, the background material on Jesus is not there, whether such additions would have made *The Passion* a better cinematic work of art or not. On this point we should probably pay attention to Ebert's remarks when he said, "I prefer to evaluate a film on the basis of what it intends to do, not on what I think it should have done."[8]

The Passion of the Christ intends to honor and glorify Christ and His salvific mission. In this sense it "preaches" the Christian message. The best-known American evangelist, Billy Graham, was so impressed by the film that he stated, "*The Passion of the Christ* is a lifetime of sermons in one movie." Cardinal Dario Castrillon Hoyos, Vatican Prefect for the Congregation of the Clergy, stated that the movie was "more effective than any sermons I'll ever preach."

Religious Ritual

Roger Ebert's comment that discussion of individual performances is beside the point is extremely important. This remark begins to penetrate the essence of the movie. Many have already referred to *The Passion* as a sermon, or experience. It is ultimately these things because of the way the movie is filmed. *The Passion*'s religious depth, its sharp theological focus, its solemnity, make it a kind of religious ritual put to film. In sacred rites, personalities do not matter. The actors, similar to participants in a religious ritual, do not dominate the film; rather the subject matter dominates them. The personality of the actors, especially Caviezel, is submerged into the role. The movie does not serve them—they serve it and become transparent so that the mysteries of faith may be expressed through them. Some film reviewers have remarked that Caviezel never really had a chance to perform. One of these critics observed:

---

[8] Ebert.

Perhaps the hardest criticism to overlook is that this movie treats Jesus as a prop. The personality of the man never has a chance to come through.

Caviezel is a talented actor, but he spends so much screen time in a semi-conscious state, under so much gore and blood, that it's impossible for him to emote. Flashback scenes show a calm and peaceful Jesus with his disciples, but these flashbacks are too short to round out the character.

Then again, perhaps Gibson and Caviezel deliberately tried to leave Jesus as a blank, allowing the audience to fill in the details from their own beliefs.[9]

It's not quite fair to say that Caviezel portrays Jesus "as a blank." He does have personality, but echoing Ebert, that's almost beside the point. On playing Jesus, Caviezel stated: "I don't want people to see me, I just want them to see Jesus."[10] The central character of the film is already known to millions of viewers. The actor best fills the role who portrays Christ in a universally recognizable and believable way—especially in a film firmly rooted in the Christian faith that intends to express that faith. It's best for Christ to come through and for the actor to just get out of the way.

The mere fact that *The Passion* is filmed in two dead languages already infuses the movie with a certain mystical sense. In an effort to recreate the historical setting of the Passion, Gibson used the languages of the time. But the languages of Latin and Aramaic—Christ's own native tongue—not only serve the goal of historical authenticity; these dead languages support the ritual dimension of the film. Latin and Aramaic are not only "dead"; they are ancient languages and they are, moreover, li-

---

[9] Mary Mapes, "The Passion of the Christ," *Movie Habit*, February 27, 2004, www.moviehabit.com.

[10] "Jim Caviezel Tells of Meeting the Pope," www.Zenit.com, March 16, 2004.

turgical languages—Latin used for two thousand years in the Roman rite of the Catholic Church and Aramaic used in the Chaldean rite of the same Church. By the fact that these languages are not simply foreign, but dead and ancient, the audience is automatically lifted out of its usual, familiar world and placed into a completely different world that is impossible to get to by boat, plane, train or car. This already is an element of ritual. Liturgical language takes the participant out of the ordinary and readies him for an experience he could not create for himself.[11]

The Passion functions as ritual because its material is directly spiritual. The movie never sidetracks to what is not spiritually focused on the Passion of the Christ. For instance there are no subplots to distract from the film's only purpose. Like ritual, the movie has a single emphasis. It is tightly woven together by biblical, liturgical, devotional, doctrinal and theological material, much of which is already very familiar and already very spiritually significant—even dear—to the Christian viewer. Like ritual, the movie makes the most sense to the initiated. The devout Christian is the privileged viewer. Those who are not Christian and those not very familiar with the Christian religion will not be able to enter into the rich theological symbolism of the movie. It is like the non-Christian or even the Protestant who is invited to attend a Catholic Mass. Such a person, suddenly thrust into a liturgical world of strange words, symbols and gestures, may be overwhelmed by it all and certainly confused—fumbling through the missalette trying to keep up. Everything needs to be explained to him as the ceremony provokes questions like, "Why do you do this?" and, "What is the meaning of that?" The newcomer may find the ritual attractive, but at the same time threat-

---

[11] For a good discussion of how language serves the ritual and mystical dimension of the film see Seth Sanders, "Mystically Correct," *Criterion* (Publication of the University of Chicago Divinity School), Spring 2004. Also at http://uchicago.edu/~sanders

ening. Often the experience of ritual will provoke the non-initi-
ated to learn more about the Christian faith.

One of the most insightful critiques of *The Passion* was
written by Richard Alleva and published in *Christianity Today*.
Alleva observed that *The Passion* is not a dramatic work of art.
Drama occurs through the conflict of decision-making. Jesus in
The Passion only struggles with a decision in the beginning of
the movie. Alleva contrasts the Gibson film with Martin
Scorsese's *The Last Temptation of Christ*, in which Jesus is the
subject of a satanic temptation, but overcomes the "devil's offer
of a normal family life" at the end of the movie. In other words,
the climax is a truly dramatic moment of the character. But
Alleva (who is not without his criticisms of *The Passion*) understands that Gibson's film operates on a different level: "In contrast to Scorsese, Gibson has elected to make a ritualistic work
rather than a dramatic one." Alleva focused on the film's very
bloody violence, but he understood why it was necessary.

> *The Passion* is not just a gruesome movie, but a ritual
> that exalts the blood of Jesus, because the release of
> this blood released humanity from sin. Those who
> charge Mel Gibson with being obsessed with blood
> and violence are correct, but they are making an idle
> point, since Gibson obviously believes that blood
> sacrifice lies at the very source of his religion. And
> since when is moderation the salient virtue of artists
> and Christians... the sacred roots of Christianity are
> not rational at all, but speak to desires within us that
> can only be satisfied by magnificence and extremity.
> *The Passion of the Christ* is soaked in blood. Ritual
> tends to be. How amazing that a ritual is now play-
> ing in multiplexes.[12]

---

[12] Richard Alleva, "Torturous, Mel Gibson's 'The Passion of the Christ,'" *Christianity Today*, March 12, 2004, Vol. 131, No. 5.

The Passion has the power to bring the viewer to a deeper awareness of the sacrifice of Christ and His great love for mankind to have endured such suffering. Many Christians read the accounts of the Passion in Scripture, and see religious paintings and crucifixes that draw them into the reality of Christ's sacrifice and its meaning. Like these things, *The Passion of the Christ* is an aid to spiritual meditation literally writ large. In this sense it is not just a movie. Christians for two millennia have meditated upon the life of Christ. This meditation involves actually imagining Jesus, His face, His gestures, His voice, imagining the biblical scene and other characters in that scene, and even placing oneself into the scene. The meditation is like a movie inside one's brain. The spiritual meditation is aided by writings of saints and mystics, religious paintings, stained glass, sculpture and music. Movies, too, can aid the spiritual journey but in this regard Gibson's film is definitely unique. Many movies aid the spiritual journey despite themselves. *The Passion* is crafted with this purpose in mind. It does not simply represent Christ's death. Like a great religious painting or piece of music, it draws the viewer into the truths of Jesus' life, death and resurrection. Like great religious art, the movie is the fruit of faith and has the ability to deepen, even awaken faith. "The film is so enthralling that perhaps some viewers will have to remind themselves that it is just a movie and not a substitute for the New Testament, much less for sacramental liturgies or the stations of the cross familiar to so many Christians during Lent."[13]

The final chapter of this book is devoted to reactions to the movie. The fact that an author can even devote an extended amount of text to discuss how a movie personally affected people's lives demonstrates that *The Passion* is not an ordinary movie. On the essence of this movie one viewer stated quite rightly:

---

[13] Hittinger and Lev.

This is not a movie that anyone will "like." I don't think it is a movie anyone will "love." It certainly does not "entertain." There isn't even the sense that one has just watched a movie. What it is, is an experience—on a level of primary emotion that is scarcely comprehensible. Every shred of human preconception is stripped away. No one will eat popcorn during this film. Some may not eat for days after they've seen it.... What Gibson has done is to use all of his considerable skill to portray the most dramatic moment of the most dramatic events since the dawn of time. There is no escape. It's a punch to the gut that puts you on the canvas, and you don't get up. You are simply confronted by the horror of what was done—and why. Throughout the entire film I found myself apologizing.[14]

I am a theologian and thus place my theological skill, knowledge and insight at the service of explaining the spiritual *meaning* of The Passion of the Christ. *The Passion* is a rare film because it is truly theological in the classical sense. The word "theology" means the study of God. Classical, authentic theology is faith seeking understanding—or intellectual worship. Though theology is often very personal, the object of study is not. In other words, the "object" of study is not anyone's private issues, but the Revelation of God. Thus the "object" of study has an objective content. *The Passion of the Christ* is a theological exploration and expression of the Revelation of God as it is given to the Church in Scripture and Sacred Tradition. It is theological in the classic sense because its producer is a believer who seeks to understand the faith as it is presented in Revelation.

---

14 "Review of 'The Passion of the Christ' by Jody Dean, [Dallas] CBS News Anchor," posted on www.grammyandpapajoe.blogspot.com, March 5, 2004.

Certainly the execution of a theological image may be dependent upon film technique. However, for the purpose of this book, the *meaning* of the image is primary, the cinematic technique secondary. The first four chapters of this book explore, examine, discuss and reveal the theological meaning of this film. The fifth chapter examines the sources for the film's theology. The final chapter is focused on why *The Passion* provokes intense reaction and just what is the nature of this reaction. An Appendix compares *The Passion* to several other cinematic treatments of the subject.

It is almost impossible to name another movie that has stimulated debates and discussions to the extent that *The Passion of the Christ* has done. In many ways this book is the result of those discussions and debates. Thousands of unprecedented Catholic and Protestant discussion groups took place in the wake of the film's Ash Wednesday 2004 opening. This alone is evidence of the movie's phenomenal nature. In addition, whole churches bought out local theaters for special showings of the movie—many of those showings preceded by speeches and workshops. Add to this the countless chat rooms on the Internet all devoted to discussion of the film. Many denominations published detailed critiques of and study guides for the movie. These things testify to the fact that *The Passion* is a phenomenon. Gibson's film is assured new generations of viewers as it will be seen in various formats (private screenings, DVD, etc.) every Lenten season well into the future. Its influence as a film and as a spiritual work of art will be felt for decades to come.

Chapter One

THE FIRST AND FINAL GOOD NEWS

HE GARDEN IS BATHED IN DARKNESS. Beams of light from the moon only occasionally pierce the black night. The white orb dodges in and out from behind the evening fog and clouds. As the dark night is pierced with faint beams of light, so the silence is pierced by the muted sounds of an anguished soul in prayer—a voice in solitude. Mel Gibson's film *The Passion of the Christ* begins in the night garden of Gethsemane. The scene is shrouded in conflict, sorrow and mystery. The lens of the camera meanders through the trees and mist like the eye of a malevolent stalker. This eye approaches the lone figure from behind. The man is in distress. He sways back and forth in anguish of soul. It is Jesus. From the start of the film He is the Christ of the Passion. The film immediately thrusts the viewer into the center of the drama of salvation.

Satan is the next character to appear. It is striking, even disturbing that the character is not just a voice, a beam of light, a bird or some other animal, but an actual *someone*—someone with whom Christ must really contend. This may be the film's first theological idea—that the Devil is real. The scene of Christ praying in the garden is of course recorded in all four Gospels. In the Gospels Christ prays: "Father, if it is your will, take this cup from me; yet not my will but yours be done" (Luke 21:42). In the first garden Satan sought out the Old Adam. Now we are

1

back in the garden and Satan seeks out the New Adam. In the first garden Satan crept into the presence of Eve and Adam. By lies and cunning he caused them to give up their identity as they refused God's will. The Devil succeeded in leading Adam, the head of the human race, away from his God-given mission. Now, as the Second Adam is on the brink of restoring what was lost by the First Adam, Satan creeps into the garden again to thwart the accomplishment of the Father's will in His Son.

Gibson's Jesus sweats blood in keeping with the biblical description: "His sweat became as drops of blood falling to the ground" (Luke 22:44). The literal Passion of Christ has already begun. The beads of blood on Jesus' forehead foreshadow the great amount of blood we will see in the film's unfolding of the Passion. The Devil tries to tempt Christ on two points: His ability to actually bear the sins of men and His identity as the Son of God. Satan asks Christ, "Who is your father?" Jesus affirms His identity. He accepts the Father's will with the words "Thy will be done." At this point dark clouds pass over the moon and all light is blotted out. Christ, when He fully accepts the salvific mission to suffer for the sins of men, is in darkness. He collapses to the ground. A real serpent is sent out from the cold, androgynous Satan. The serpent slides across the ground and rests on Jesus' hand. Christ raises Himself up. Without hesitation Christ crushes the serpent with one powerful blow of His foot. The viewer is jolted by this unexpected and absolutely firm and resolute action on the part of Jesus. With this gesture the prologue of the movie is over and the action of the Passion is immediately ushered in. Judas and the Temple guards arrive to arrest Jesus.

The film's theological foundation is set when Gibson opens the movie with Christ, Satan, and the garden. It is the recapitulation of what is known as the Protoevangelium, the Latin term for "First Good News" or "Proto Gospel." It is found in Genesis 3:15. After the sin of Adam and Eve, God addresses the serpent:

> I will put enmity between you and the woman,
> > and between your offspring and hers;
> He will strike at your head,
> > while you strike at his heel.

Jesus is the Offspring of the woman—the New Adam who will render the mortal blow to the Devil's head. Thus in the dark night of Eden is the bright promise of salvation. The woman's Offspring has arrived in the fulfillment of the Proto Gospel. Genesis 3:15 is an important and primary theological key to Gibson's film. Indeed, the drama of the Proto Gospel is played out in the movie from the beginning scene all the way to the film's end with the vanquishing of Satan.

The Passion of the Christ (and Mary)

Unlike any other film depiction of Jesus, Mary is central to the drama of Gibson's film. Mary's role in the drama of salvation is one of the most profound theological statements of the movie. For some Protestant viewers of the movie, it is also one of the most controversial. A Protestant Evangelical pastor in Wisconsin wrote his own review of the film and sent it out to his email list. Entitled "The Passion of the Christ or The Emperor's New Clothes," the pastor tells us how he had hoped for a biblically faithful rendering of the Christ story. He left the theater disappointed and stated: "They should have named the film 'The Passion of Christ *and Mary*.'" He laments that the movie "is fraught with an unbiblical fixation on Mary, the mother of Jesus." Of course, many other Protestants have viewed the film and found it an edifying spiritual experience—despite or perhaps even because of the movie's so-called "non-biblical" obsession with Mary.

Not only is Christ the New Adam of the Proto Gospel, but the character of Mary is interpreted by Gibson through the lens

3

of Genesis 3:15. This is one of the movie's rich theological insights. The Proto Gospel states that God will place enmity between the serpent "and the woman." Eve will give birth to an Offspring. This first prophecy of the Old Testament thrusts us into the future when the Offspring shall be born who crushes Satan's head. Thus we are pointed, not only to the New Adam, but also to the New Eve. The Proto Gospel affirms that redemption is the work of the woman and her Offspring. Together they do battle with the Evil One. A Catholic Church document called *Munificentissimus Deus* (an Apostolic Constitution issued by Pope Pius XII on November 1, 1950) stated:

> We must remember especially that, since the second century, the Virgin Mary has been designated by the holy Fathers as the New Eve, who, although subject to the New Adam, is most intimately associated with Him in that struggle with the infernal foe which, as foretold in the Protoevangelium (Genesis 3:15), finally resulted in the most complete victory over sin and death.

Gibson might as well have had this document open on his lap when making the movie. According to Genesis 3:15, the Adversary of the New Adam is the Adversary of the Woman. Therefore the mother of the Offspring does not stand idle in her Son's Passion. She actually contributes to the overcoming of the Evil One. In Gibson's movie the characters of the Proto Gospel take their places in the Passion. The observation of Christian scholar F.M. Braun can be applied to this film: The crucifixion is the great battleground in which all the traits of the Proto Gospel come together.[1] In *The Passion of the Christ* all the great personages of

---

[1] F.M. Braun, *La Mere des fideles*, Casterman-Tournai: Cahiers de L'Actutalité Religieuse, 1954, p. 91.

the messianic drama meet each other for the final and definitive contest.

Mary, in the Gibson film, is the only other character, besides Christ, who actually sees Satan. The beaten and bleeding Christ is carrying His cross through a street in Jerusalem. Mary follows along on one side of the street. Satan walks silently and unnoticed on the other side. In the noisy crowd gathered to watch the criminal walk to his execution, Mary alone sees the Devil. Their eyes meet. The moment of the ancient enmity has arrived. This scene in Gibson's film shows that Mary and Satan are in contention. Satan stares at Mary with a look of "I dare you." Satan is there to mock, deride and demoralize Christ—to seek after and work for His fall.

Mary is there to support her Son, even to protect Him and to aid Him to accomplish His salvific task. Indeed, almost as soon as Mary sees the Evil One she turns her attention back to Jesus almost as if she were aware of the danger to her Son by the presence of Satan. It is then that Mary asks John to find a way to bring her closer to Christ.

The Demon Child

One of the most disturbing and even perplexing satanic images in the movie occurs during the scourging of Christ at the pillar. The soldiers switch from beating Christ with rods to beating Him with cat-o'-nine-tails. At this point Satan appears for the second time in the movie. The Evil One literally slides across the screen behind those who view the beating. As she slides across the screen the viewer sees that she is carrying a child. The Devil gradually unwraps the child and reveals him to the viewer. The head of the child turns around to face the audience. He is very large for a child. His arms and back have dark hair and he has a large, squarish, almost adult-sized head. The child clings to Satan as a child clings to his mother. He even caresses Satan's cheek. He looks at Christ being mercilessly beaten and smiles grotesquely and hideously. What is the meaning of this odd scene? The Proto Gospel provides the theological context for it: "I will place enmity between you and the woman, between your offspring and hers." The Devil has offspring. Satan holding the demon child is a sick parody of the truth of Mary and Christ. The Devil often tries to imitate the truth of God to lure people away from it—this is the counterfeit mother and child. This satanic mother and child appear together in a fond, tender embrace when Christ and Mary cannot embrace. The satisfaction, comfort and closeness that the satanic mother and child express is what the world prefers to the separation, torture and suffering of the other Mother and Child—the kind of life you get when you are involved in the plan of God.

The image of the Devil's offspring operates on more than one level. On one level the image appears when it does as a kind of taunt to Mary. Satan can comfort her child—Mary cannot comfort hers. But it is not just a matter of comfort. Mary cannot put Christ into a safe place as the Devil can do with her child. Moreover, because Mary is actively involved in the salvific acts of her Son—acts that cause Him to suffer, Mary, from Satan's point of view, is a failure as a mother. Mary's mission as the New Eve is to aid her Son to fulfill the Father's will, and thus go to the cross. In the Devil's mind, if Mary can be lured away from her role as the New Eve to the New Adam, Christ will not be able to undergo His Passion. As the New Eve, Mary must at least accept that her Son will suffer, if not in fact help Jesus go to the cross. The Devil's child confronts us with a mystery about motherhood. Mary, as the New Eve must allow her Son to suffer— has to let go of her Son if He would accomplish His mission as the New Adam. But, often this letting go is the hardest thing a mother can do. Mothers often prefer to cling to their children, protect them—hold them back from danger. At certain stages in a child's life a mother's comfort is necessary, but when a mother continues to comfort her child in the wrong way this can interfere with the development of the child who may never come to maturity. The child can never really become an adult son or daughter of God. Mary comforts Christ in *The Passion* but her comfort is not given to save Him from suffering, but to enable Him to endure it.

The demon child is very big. What child this huge would be held like a tiny baby unless it was a child prevented from growing up? If the child cannot grow up he cannot assume his God-given mission. This satanic mother and her baby are what the Devil wants Mary and Christ to be. If Satan can get Mary to be a clinging mother, then Christ's mission might be thwarted. The Devil is there with her demon child as the reverse and opposite image of Mary and Christ. Mary and Christ fulfill the real meaning of Mother and Child in the salvific plan of God for the world.

When Jesus is presented with the cross of rough-hewn wood He prays: "Father, I am ready. I am your son and the son of your handmaid." It is very interesting that Mary is included in this prayer of Christ as He prepares to walk the dolorous path to the crucifixion. Christ not only identifies Himself as the Son of the Father, but Mary is included in the mystery of her Son in the accomplishment of His mission—a declaration that He is both God and Man.

Mary affirmed her own identity as the "handmaid of the Lord" when she accepted to be the Mother of God. The Mary of Gibson's film is the Mary of the "yes," the Mary who utters the "*fiat mihi.*" "Let it be done to me," she said to the angel who announced to her that she would conceive the Son of God by the power of the Holy Spirit (Luke 1:35). The Mary of *The Passion* demonstrates a mystical unity with Jesus. She is aware of Him and aware of His suffering even when she cannot see Him. After Jesus is arrested in the garden, bound with chains and led off by the Temple guard, one of the guards renders Christ a vicious blow. The scene immediately cuts to Mary who suddenly is jerked out of her sleep, as if her Son having been struck awakened her. This blow is the first of many and in a sense the Passion of Christ is officially ushered in by it. Mary is aware that this night will be unlike any other. She is already tuned in to the suffering of her Son. When Christ, whose face the blows of the Temple guards have already disfigured, is taken to the Sanhedrin, Mary sees her Son and says, "It has begun." She adds, "So be it." The Mary who said "yes" to the Incarnation is the Mary who now says "yes" to the sacrifice of Christ in her continued self-surrender to the plan of God.

The Gibson film provides us with another perplexing scene. Mary is present during Christ's trial before the Sanhedrin. After Caiaphas has convicted Jesus of blasphemy, the crowds finally disperse and there is a time of quiet. Mary, John and Mary Magdalen enter an open courtyard. Mary seems to be listening for something and looking about the open court space. She leaves the company of John and Mary Magdalen. The audience is not quite sure what she is doing. She alone seems to be aware of something. Mary then kneels down on the pavement and presses her eye into a crack between the stones. The camera takes you below the stones to Jesus who is chained directly beneath her. He looks up, aware of her presence. Though the cold stone may separate them, their spiritual destinies are one. Mary is not only the physical Mother of Christ, but she is spiritually linked to Him as well. By this bond she has the power to find Him. As the Mother of the Redeemer, Mary comes in Christ's darkest Hour to strengthen Him in His mission. Mary was not simply the passive instrument of the Incarnation, nor is she the passive onlooker of the Passion of her Son. Mary helps Christ accomplish the work of salvation.

Mary Holds Christ Up

The Roman soldiers have beaten Jesus with rods. The beating is filmed in its entire graphic brutality and cruelty. Christ's hands, bloody and black with sweat, shake uncontrollably from the pain. The beating has brought Him to His knees. Jesus looks at Mary and she looks at Him. Suddenly Jesus begins to rise to His feet and with great effort He stands erect. The Roman soldiers are amazed. They have never seen anything like this. Indeed, they exclaim in Latin: "Impossible!" "Incredible!" Christ was able to stand up after such torture because Mary's glance confirmed Him. One might want to ask: Why should Christ stand up? Why would He even want to stand up? Wouldn't it be better to show the guards that He can't take any more punishment? Indeed, when Christ raises Himself up this prompts the soldiers to apply even more torture and so the beating shifts from rods to cat-o'-nine-tails.

When Christ stands up, the film is making a theological statement. Jesus is in charge of His sacrifice, not Caiaphas or Pilate or the soldiers beating Him. This episode illustrates the words of Jesus when He said: "The Father loves me for this; that I lay down my life to take it up again. No one takes it from me; I lay it down freely. I have the power to lay it down, and I have the power to take it up again" (John 10:18).

When Jesus reaches Calvary His mother again strengthens Him. When Jesus arrives, He is half-dead with exhaustion. Upon reaching the summit He collapses. The soldiers order Him to get up but He cannot. Mary is at the edge of the crowd. Jesus sees her. As at Christ's scourging at the pillar, so here their eyes meet. After Jesus sees Mary He gets up again. The presence of His mother has once again given Him the strength to go to the cross.

Gibson's Mary does not simply watch her Son offer His sacrifice for the sins of the world. This Mary is very different from

9

the memorable Mary of Franco Zeffirelli's *Jesus of Nazareth* played by Olivia Hussey. In the Zeffirelli film Mary is quite passive at the crucifixion and can do nothing but weep and mourn the torture and death of her Son. All that she can do is receive the dead body of her Son after it is all over. She rocks him back and forth as she wails in terrible grief. As Jesus' mother, her primary role is to be a figure of pity and through her the viewer of the film is drawn into the great sorrow of the crucifixion. Nearly every film depiction of Mary follows this pattern.

The Mary of *The Passion* is most certainly a Mary filled with grief but she is also a Mary of great courage. This is a Mary who takes the initiative, a Mary who takes risks, a Mary who, though she has moments of hesitation, is overall a Mary who is bold and can overcome her fears. This is a Mary very actively engaged in her Son's salvific task. As the New Eve, who will undo the "knot of Eve's disobedience," as St. Irenaeus taught, Mary is completely focused on Christ and His mission and is His aid and support in the accomplishment of the Father's will.

The very moving scene between Jesus and His mother on the Via Dolorosa perhaps definitively demonstrates Mary's active role in Christ's mission. Jesus is carrying His cross. After Mary sees Satan she is desperate to be close to her Son and she asks John to find her a way to be near Him. John, Mary and Mary Magdalen swiftly go around the crowd and down a narrow street. Mary suddenly holds back. She is filled with dread to continue. Jesus appears at the end of the street, His strength crushed by the weight of the cross. He collapses and the cross falls on top of Him. Mary sees Him crash to the ground.

Many viewers count what happens next as the most moving scene of the whole film. A flashback takes us to the time when Jesus was a small boy. While running He falls and hurts Himself. Mary rushes to Him to comfort Him. She rocks Him in her arms and assures Him: "I'm here." On the side street Mary is strengthened by this memory. As she comforted Jesus then, she must do so now. Mary rushes to Her bleeding and beaten Son. Leaving the side street she bursts through the crowd and falls on the Via Dolorosa where her Son has fallen. Mary has left the "side-street" of her own emotional hesitation to join Jesus in the very center of the path of suffering. She embraces Jesus and assures Him: "I'm here!" By these words He is again strengthened. Jesus' hand touches Mary's face and He cries out to her: "See, Mother, I make all things new." With these words Christ summons all His strength, picks up the cross and continues on the path to Calvary. If one looks closely one can see Mary raise her hands up slightly, as if she were helping Jesus to get up.

It might be argued here that Gibson's portrayal of Mary is simply that of a mother showing concern for her child. It is true that Mary's concern is certainly borne out of her maternal love for Jesus. However, this does not explain why Jesus responds to her presence with renewed resolve to continue. Mary's presence directly affects the fulfillment of His salvific task. Her maternal relationship to Him is not simply a biological motherhood. Mary's motherhood intimately connects her to Christ not only on a natural level, but her maternal bond is taken into the sphere of His redemptive mission and her maternal love is directed towards helping Jesus accomplish the will of the Father.

Mary's presence to Christ links Him to His mission. In a real sense she is the fulfillment of the Letter to the Hebrews when it states: "'A body you have prepared for me'...we have been sanctified through the offering of the body of Christ once for all" (Heb 10:5, 10). Mary links Christ to the very reason He became man—to be that perfect offering to the Father. Mary said "yes" to God for a reason—to make historically tangible the One who will "save his people from their sins" (Mt 1:21). Mary's presence to Jesus is an affirmation of who He is, because His reason to be is her reason to be as well. When Christ fulfills His mission He fulfills Mary's. His sacrifice is the very meaning of her maternity. The Word became Flesh to offer His life for the salvation of the world. Mary strengthens Christ in the very moment of His offering because she is the Mother of the Word made Flesh.

"See I make all things new." This line in the film is connected to the first flashback of the movie. In this scene Jesus and Mary are at home in the days prior to Christ's public ministry. By this flashback we are given a glimpse of the warmth, joy, happiness and intimacy of Jesus and Mary and the very human love of a mother and her son.

In the flashback Jesus is engaged in the carpenter's trade making a table. But this is an unusual sort of table. This is a tall table and it will need tall chairs. The table is very different. Indeed it is new. Mary comes out to investigate it and remarks that no one uses these kinds of tables and in the one line of the film that elicits at least a few chuckles from the audience, Mary says: "It'll never catch on." This is a humorous line because, while in the ancient Mid-East people ate reclining, nowadays nearly everyone in the world uses "tall" tables.

Even as a carpenter Jesus "makes all things new." The scene, through the wood of the new table, is symbolically connected to the ultimate work of the carpenter from Nazareth—the Son of Mary will, indeed, make all things new through the wood of the cross.

Chapter Two

THE MOTHER OF THE LIVING

The Passion of the Christ is built upon the Passion narratives of the four Gospels of the New Testament. However, because this movie is a cinematic theological commentary on the *meaning* of the Passion and the Christian religion, Gibson makes use of what might be termed "extra-biblical" words, gestures and symbols. Some of this material is within the Sacred Tradition of the Catholic Church. Mary, for example, is specifically called "Mother" by the disciples of Jesus. John refers to Mary this way and so does Peter.

It is not odd that Jesus calls Mary "Mother," but why should the disciples call Mary by this name? As we discussed in the first chapter, Mary is a partner with Jesus in His Passion—not a passive bystander. When Mary accepts the words of the angel to be the mother of Christ she becomes the mother of Christ on the cross. Thus when she gives birth to Jesus she gives birth to all those who will be reborn by the blood of His sacrifice. When the disciples call Mary "Mother" they recognize that, as the mother of the Redeemer, she is their mother too. Furthermore, by having the disciples call Mary by the title of "Mother," Gibson is making another theological statement. As the New Eve, Mary stands in relation to the New Adam as a sign of the Church.

Peter's Confession

After Peter denies Christ three times it is significant that he immediately runs into Mary in the courtyard. Peter is consumed with grief, guilt and remorse. Instead of running away or hiding himself from Mary, he falls at her feet. Mary sees his distress and looks upon him, even touches him, compassionately. With eyes full of tears Peter tells her explicitly his sin: "I have denied Him, Mother. Denied Him three times." He then yells, "I'm not worthy," and runs off. The audience is left hanging, as the character of Peter is never seen again. The viewer is left to fill in the result of Peter's repentance. Except for those who know absolutely nothing about Christianity, it is understood that his repentance was fruitful and that Peter took his place as head of the Church. This is a good example of how the initiated are the privileged viewers of the film.

It is significant in Gibson's film that Peter goes to Mary. The declaration of his guilt to her is the equivalent of a confession. His sin is confessed to the Church. In this, guilt is brought where it needs to be brought. Peter's sinfulness is brought to the only place that could bear such a confession—to the heart of Mary, the heart of the Church. It doesn't matter that Peter is still in agony and dashes off. He has revealed the truth of his soul to the Mother of all Christians, a sign of the Church, and with that Gibson has made his theological point.

Judas and His Despair

Immediately after Peter confesses to Mary, the film switches to Judas—the other disciple who has sinned against Jesus. While Gibson's Peter is racked with remorse and deep grief, Judas is a figure completely tortured in soul. After Peter confesses to Mary, Judas seeks out the Sanhedrin. Judas tries to make amends for his sin and seeks relief from the wrong he has done. He enters the presence of Caiaphas, Annas and other priests and elders and tells them to release Jesus, that he has betrayed an innocent man. He begs them to take back the money that he was paid for his betrayal of Christ. Caiaphas tells him that if he thinks he has betrayed an innocent man that is Judas's problem. Unlike Peter who confesses his sin to the Church in the person of Mary, Judas seeks to reclaim his soul through the representatives of the Law, the Prophets, and the Temple who, while they certainly will not give him absolution, in essence *cannot* give it. This is part of an overall theological statement that *The Passion of the Christ* makes about Judaism in relation to Christianity. We will take a closer look at this issue in Chapter Four.

Unlike nearly every movie made about Jesus since 1960, *The Passion* does not subject the character of Judas to psychoanalysis. The movie does not get inside of Judas's head. Instead, it gets inside of his soul. To be sure, Judas in *The Passion* is a character to be pitied, but not pitied because he was really just a confused good guy. One reason he is an object of absolute pity is because Judas seeks relief for his soul in the wrong place and cannot find it. Not only does he go to the keepers of the Old Law to get it—Judas tries to erase his sin by his own powers. Judas constantly wipes his mouth. He wipes his lips with the back of his hand after he sees the bloodied and bruised face of Jesus who has fallen over the bridge. He wipes them against the rough stone of a pillar and then on the sleeve of his cloak as he watches Jesus' trial before the Sanhedrin. He gashes his mouth with the moneybag full of silver that the chief priests refuse to take back. In this gesture two things come together: the payment for the betrayal and the instrument of the betrayal. By the time Judas commits suicide his mouth is swollen, pitted, bloody and full of sores.

One of the witnesses at the trial accuses Jesus of telling people that He will give them His flesh to eat. It is interesting to note that when the witness speaks these words the camera is focused on Judas who scrapes his mouth against the pillar and wipes it on his sleeve. The mouth that kissed Jesus in betrayal is unworthy to receive the Eucharistic flesh of Jesus. He tries to wipe the guilt away.

The film does not provide a specific reason why Judas betrayed Jesus. But Gibson does provide a broader reason and ultimately the more spiritually important reason. Judas is a character on the side of Satan. Besides Jesus and Mary, Judas is the only character in the film that Satan and his demons pay any attention to. The Gospel of John provides several reasons why Judas betrayed Christ. The first has to do with Judas's lack of faith. In chapter 6 of John's Gospel, Jesus had told His disciples, "'Unless you eat the flesh of the Son of Man and drink His blood, you do not have life within you....' Many of his disciples who were listening said, 'This teaching is hard: who can accept it?' Jesus... said to them... 'The words I speak to you are Spirit and life. But there are some of you who don't believe.' For Jesus knew from the beginning who they were who didn't believe, and who it was who would hand him over" (John 6:53-65).

Another reason was Judas's own personal lack of character. In chapter 12 of John's Gospel Mary Magdalen anoints Jesus with a very costly aromatic nard. Judas criticizes this extravagance saying that the money could have been used for the poor. But John says that Judas was not concerned for the poor. John calls Judas a thief who "held the purse, and used to help himself to what was deposited there" (John 12:6).

The last reason is even more to the point. John 13:2 states: "The Devil had already induced Judas, son of Simon Iscariot, to hand [Jesus] over." Later in verse 27 we are told that Satan entered Judas's heart.

The Judas of the Gibson film is a tortured figure in the hands of Satan and his demons. He is tormented by demons and he tries to flee them. After Judas's failed attempt to take back

16

his betrayal of Jesus, he is seen sitting in the dark on the side of a street. He looks pathetic and desolate and his condition draws the attention of two children playing with a ball. They show concern for him. They soon notice that there is something wrong with his mouth. Instead of accepting the children's concern for him and being drawn into their pity for him, Judas tells the children to leave him alone and calls them "little devils." At this point the children turn on him and remark that "a curse is inside of him." The faces of the children turn grotesque and ugly. Judas does not see them as caring, innocent children. Indeed, he sees them as "little devils." Judas's sin and his inability to seek relief in the right places causes him to see everything in a distorted fashion. In *A Guide to the Passion* published by Ascension Press and Catholic Exchange, the authors state that "To portray such innocent children at play in such a twisted and terrifying manner underscores the consequences of sin twisting our perception of the good, the true and the beautiful."

The next time we see Judas he is being driven out of town by a band of angry children wild with rage, who spit and throw rocks at him. The figure of Satan stands behind the children. Then suddenly the children are gone. They seem to just vanish. The curse is within Judas, not outside of him. He is quite alone now. He was one of those called by Christ to be a disciple—one of the Twelve—but in his sin and his inability to be rid of it Judas has no company, no society.

The Carcass

Judas notices something behind him and he slowly, and with deep apprehension, turns around. Here one of the most troubling images in the Gibson film appears. On the ground lies a dead and decaying carcass of a donkey—still with a tether rope around his head. The carcass, stiff with death and filled with maggots, appears to have been abandoned. He was once part of something—now he's not. Judas looks at this lifeless creature in horror. What does this image mean?

The dead and decaying carcass serves as an image of Judas's own soul. When Judas sees this reflection he is driven to ultimate despair. In the next scene Judas ties the dead donkey's tether rope around the branch of a nearby tree and hangs himself. The instrument of his suicide, by the way, is mentioned in the Douay/Rheims version of the Gospel of Matthew: "he... went away and hanged himself with a halter" (Matthew 27:5). As his body dangles from the branch we see the dead carcass in the background. The death in this animal is transferred to him— the outcast nature of this beast is his own. Judas, who could not erase his sin, is erased from the company of men. In the end he erases himself.

There's something else we might consider about this carcass. Jews do not allow dead things to just lie around. It is important in Judaism not to come into contact with the dead—to touch or be touched by dead things. For example, the Book of Leviticus 22:4-5 states: "If anyone touches a person who has become unclean by contact with a corpse... that one shall be unclean until evening and may not eat of the sacred portions until he has bathed his body in water; then when the sun sets, he again becomes clean. Only then may be eat of the sacred offerings, which are his food."

The image of the dead and decaying donkey is an image of Judas's outcast soul. By a sin he cannot expiate Judas is an outcast from both the community of men and the community of God. He is forever cut off from the worship of God—never to eat the sacred offerings. His mouth cannot touch the Eucharist.

The scene of Judas's despair was inspired by the visions of Blessed Anne Catherine Emmerich, a 19th century Catholic mystic and visionary whose work *The Dolorous Passion of Our Lord*

Jesus Christ is a key source for Gibson's film. We will consider her in more detail in Chapter Five. Emmerich states:

> I again beheld him rushing to and fro like a madman in the valley of Hinnom: Satan was by his side in a hideous form, whispering in his ear, to endeavor to drive him to despair, all the curses which the prophets had hurled upon this valley, where the Jews had formerly sacrificed their children to idols.

The valley she describes was a real place. 2 Kings 16:13 states that King Ahaz, terror-stricken at the threat of the Syro-Israelite alliance, "burned his son as an offering in the Valley of Hinnom just outside the city [of Jerusalem]." This valley is also called "Gehenna"—associated with hell in the New Testament. Regarding Judas, Emmerich saw:

> It appeared that all these maledictions were directed against [Judas], as in these words, for instance: "They shall go forth, and behold the carcasses of those who have sinned against me, whose worm dieth not, and whose fire shall never be extinguished."

Emmerich describes the Valley of Hinnom as "a dreary, desolate spot filled with rubbish and putrid remains." In her vision Satan continues to torment Judas with the words: "They are now about to put him to death; thou hast sold him. Knowest thou not the words of the law: 'He who selleth a soul among his brethren, and receiveth the price of it, let him die the death.'"

Mary—Sign of the Church

The Passion of the Christ does not manipulate the audience to despise Judas for his betrayal of Christ. After all, his betrayal is the story of mankind. The focus of the Judas character is on his total guilt and his despair in the face of it. As we mentioned earlier, Peter falls at the feet of Mary and confesses his sin—a scene also inspired by Emmerich's *Dolorous Passion*. Mary, as sign of the Church, is the center of reconciliation. It is very significant, for instance, that Cassius, the Roman soldier who converts at the end of the film, is drawn into the grace of Christ by first being drawn to Mary.[1] After Mary embraces Jesus on the Via Dolorosa and tells Him, "I'm here," this soldier is attracted to her. He asks another soldier who this woman is. The other soldier tells him that she is the "Galilean's mother"—in effect, dismissing her as a nobody—just the mother of a condemned man. Nonetheless, it is clear from the expression on Cassius' face that he is in awe of this woman.

When Mary begins to walk towards her Son dying on the cross, Cassius steps aside for her—a definite gesture of respect. When he is about to thrust the lance into Christ's side he first looks at Mary almost as if asking her if this was all right in concern for her reaction. At the end of the film he is one of those in the company of the saints gathered together around Mary and her Son at the foot of the cross. Mary will draw the outcasts in.

When Mary approaches Christ she cries out to Him: "Flesh of my flesh, heart of my heart. My Son, let me die with you." She then tenderly places her mouth to His feet and kisses them. When she pulls away we see Christ's blood upon her lips. This is one of the most significant gestures in the film. Some may wish to conclude that Mary's words and this kiss are simply the natural response any mother would make if her child were con-

---

[1] In the film Cassius makes for an odd soldier. First he has a rather puny physique and exhibits a lack of confidence. The character in the movie comes from Emmerich's *Dolorous Passion*. Their names are the same though Emmerich notes that Longinus was his baptismal name. In tradition the soldier, who in Scripture converted at the cross, is Saint Longinus. Emmerich says that Cassius was a subaltern officer, about twenty-five years of age, "whose weak squinting eyes and nervous manner had often excited the derision of his companions."

demned to die such a hideous death. However, to interpret such words and the kiss as simply the natural love of a mother for her son is to miss the Marian context of this film. Mary is not only the natural mother of Jesus in this movie. She is the New Eve and the Mother of all the living. As soon as Mary kisses Jesus, He addresses His mother and John from the cross: "Woman behold your son. Son, behold your mother." The Gospel of John (19:25-27) records the event this way:

> Near the cross of Jesus stood his mother, his mother's sister, Mary the wife of Clopas, and Mary Magdalen. Seeing his mother there with the disciple whom he loved, Jesus said to his mother, "Woman, there is your son." In turn he said to the disciple, "There is your mother."

In *The Passion* Mary's maternity is not only towards her Son, it is towards the disciples of her Son. From the cross the New Adam, who earlier in the film literally crushed the head of the serpent, accomplishes salvation in relation to the New Eve. Mary is not only the natural mother of Jesus. She is the proto-Church and as the proto-Church Mary shares in the sufferings of Christ. The Mary of the Gibson film is remarkable. She consents to the cross (as she consented to be the mother of Jesus), she is mystically connected to Him, she is a threat to Satan, her presence gives Jesus strength to endure the Passion, she is actively involved, totally engaged in the salvific work of Jesus and she suffers with Him. Mel Gibson stated in a March 2004 *Christianity Today* interview that Mary "is a tremendous co-redemptrix and mediatrix." Certainly *The Passion of the Christ* brings its depiction of Mary to the very edge of a co-redemptrix theology without an overt declaration. It is not clear what Mel Gibson understands by the term "co-redemptrix." Nonetheless, in this film Mary is definitely a partner with Christ in His Passion.

The New Testament Evidence

Is this depiction of Mary theologically justified or is the Gibson Mary, while certainly pietistic, nonetheless a biblically false mother of Jesus? The Mary who is actively involved in the Passion of Christ is justified from at least three scriptural references. The first is the prophecy of Simeon to Mary at the presentation of Jesus in the Temple. The incident is recorded in the Gospel of Luke (2:34-35):

> Simeon blessed them and said to Mary, his mother: "This child is destined to be the downfall and the rise of many in Israel, a sign that shall be opposed—and you yourself shall be pierced with a sword—so the thoughts of many hearts may be laid bare."

Simeon foretells the suffering of the Messiah. Mary is linked to that suffering. Joseph is with Mary, but Simeon's prophecy is directed specifically toward her. The Passion of Christ will involve her in a special way and she is linked to it in a way that goes beyond her, that has a significance beyond herself. Certainly any loving mother's heart would be pierced by a sword to see her child suffer cruel and completely unjust punishment. But through Mary's suffering "the thoughts of many hearts will be laid bare." When Mary endures the Passion of Christ, her suffering has an effect for others. In union with her Son's salvific suffering Mary will become a spiritual center.

The great French theologian André Feuillet states:

> "And thine own soul a sword shall pierce that out of many hearts thoughts may be revealed." So, then, the Virgin Mary is not only, together with Jesus, victim of men's opposition to the Messiah, but she is even in some way connected to the messianic judgment. Could St. Luke have more strongly made the point

that the suffering endured on Calvary by the Mother of Jesus constitutes, in its own way, an intrinsic part of the history of salvation?[2]

The great opposition that Christ will experience, as foretold by Simeon passes through the heart of Mary. Feuillet states that for Luke, "The Passion of Jesus and the compassion of his Mother are contemplated here *as a single martyrdom*" (emphasis in the original).[3]

Feuillet's point of view finds support from Pope Benedict XV's *Inter Sodalicia*:

> To such an extent did [Mary] suffer and almost die with her suffering and dying Son, and to such an extent did she surrender her maternal rights over her Son for man's salvation, and immolated Him, insofar as she could, in order to appease the justice of God, that we may rightly say that she redeemed the human race together with her Son.

Mary's intimate participation in the sacrifice of Christ renders her the supreme disciple. By the measure of her intimate experience of the Passion all men will be measured and judged. The innermost secrets of every human heart shall be laid bare in the light of her discipleship. How appropriate then that the sad and terrible measure of Peter's discipleship was laid bare to Mary in Gibson's film. By the truth of her discipleship, in which the maternal heart of Mary was opened to the world, the hearts of all men may reveal themselves as they reveal themselves in the center of the Church's maternal care for souls.

---

[2] André Feuillet, *Jesus and His Mother*, St. Bede's Publications, Still River, MA, 1984, p. 52.

[3] Ibid., p. 51.

Mary at Cana

Mary's role in the sacrifice of Christ is demonstrated at the wedding at Cana. Here we see that Mary really aids Christ in His salvific work. The account of the wedding at Cana reveals very clearly that Mary instigates the mission of her Son and thus leads Him to His Passion.

> On the third day there was a wedding at Cana in Galilee, and the mother of Jesus was there. Jesus and his disciples were likewise invited to the celebration. At a certain point the wine ran out and Jesus' mother told him, "They have no more wine." Jesus replied, "Woman, how does this concern of yours involve me? My hour has not yet come." His mother instructed those waiting on table, "Do whatever he tells you" (John 2:1-5).

The text indicates that Mary takes the initiative in the situation. She makes the lack of wine her concern and the concern of her Son. However, the miracle Mary asks of Jesus is not just a matter of replenishing a beverage. The words of Jesus to Mary are very theologically significant: "My hour has not yet come." In the Gospel of John "the hour" refers to Christ's crucifixion and to His eventual entering into His glory. In John 12 some Greek-speaking Jews come to see Jesus, and Jesus sees in these Jews from outside Israel a sign that His hour has arrived: "The hour has come for the Son of Man to be glorified" (John 12:23). Jesus then states that "unless the grain of wheat falls to the earth and dies it remains just a grain of wheat. But if it dies it produces much fruit" (v. 24). This is a direct reference to Jesus' own death. Jesus' words at Cana: "My hour has not yet come," connect His first miracle to His Passion. To perform this miracle is to usher in "the hour" which is precisely why He was conceived and "born of woman."

At Cana Mary is not only the mother of Jesus, she is the mother of His mission. She is the source, the instigator, and the principal earthly agent in bringing Christ to His public ministry. The English translation of the original Greek does not convey the full Marian significance of the miracle at Cana. When Christ objects to the miracle He states: "What [is this] to me and to you, woman? Not yet is come the hour of me." The Greek text places Jesus and Mary together in regards to the significance of the miracle. Christ's hour—Christ's Passion, in other words—encompasses them both. Mary as the woman of the hour officiates at Cana to help her Son accomplish the work of redemption for which He was conceived and brought into the world. In the miracle of Cana Jesus calls Mary "woman." He calls her "woman" again when she is at the cross fulfilling what it means for her to be the woman of the Proto Gospel—"the mother of all the living."

At Cana Mary actively serves as the catalyst of the salvific activity of her Son. Furthermore she is the cause of the revelation of His glory which is the ultimate result of the miracle. The power and glory of Christ belong to Him because He is the Son of God. But as Mary brings Christ into the world, here she causes Christ's glory to be manifested to the world. And so she is mother of the disciples' faith that comes as a result of the revelation of Christ's glory (John 2:11).

Christ executes His first miracle because someone requested it. But this someone is not just anyone—it is His mother. And it is precisely because Mary is His mother, the source of His presence in the world for the purpose of redemption, that she can ask Him for it and lead her Son to His mission. Because she is the Mother of God she has been entrusted with aiding Christ in His work of salvation. She can send Christ to the cross because she is the source of His priesthood and thus she has a maternal right to nourish its fulfillment.

For Mary to be true to her motherhood she must be true

to the salvific work of her Son. In this way Mary undoes the knot of Eve's disobedience, as St. Irenaeus taught in his theology of the New Eve. Eve led Adam away from what it meant for him to be a son of God. Eve brought Adam under the power of her own whim. The New Eve uses her authority to lead her Son, not to do her will, but the will of the Father who sent Him.

In *The Passion of the Christ*, Mary, who enters the Passion with the words, "So be it," is the enabler of Christ in the accomplishment of the Passion in contrast to Satan who seeks to divert Christ from His redemptive task.

The Woman of the Apocalypse

Finally, we should take a look at Revelation, chapter 12. Here Mary is shown as a type of the Church. Indeed the reality of Mary and the Church is nearly indistinguishable.

> A great sign appeared in the sky, a woman clothed with the sun, with the moon under her feet, and on her head a crown of twelve stars. Because she was with child she wailed aloud in pain as she labored to give birth. Then another sign appeared in the sky; it was a huge dragon.... Then the dragon stood before the woman about to give birth, ready to devour her child when it should be born. She gave birth to a son—a boy destined to shepherd all nations with an iron rod. Her child was caught up to God and to his throne....
>
> When the dragon saw that he had been cast down to the earth, he pursued the woman who had given birth to the boy. But the woman was given the wings of a gigantic eagle so that she could fly off to her place in the desert, where far from the serpent, she could be taken care of for a year and for two and a half years more. Enraged at her escape, the dragon went off to

make war on the rest of her offspring, on those who keep God's commandments and give witness to Jesus (Revelation 12:1-5, 13-15, 17.)

The woman of the Apocalypse of John is Mary who gives birth to a single child—to Christ, the Messiah King. Feuillet states:

> ...the Virgin Mary is portrayed as crowned, it is because she has triumphed over the devil whose assaults fill chapter 12; her crown is made up of 12 stars, which call to mind the 12 tribes of the New Israel, because her triumph is in some way that of the Church. If the Woman of the Apocalypse is already crowned at the very time she is giving birth to Christ (here the metaphorical childbearing of the Passion), this astounding paradox is intended to highlight the fact that the Mother of Christ, through a quite extraordinary anticipation, participates in the victory of Christ over the powers of evil, even before the Passion and the Resurrection of Christ.[4]

Revelation 12 parallels Genesis 3:15, the Proto Gospel. The Offspring of the Woman is the seed that will crush the head of the serpent. The great first prophecy of salvation finds fulfillment here. The entire chapter is filled with tension, conflict and struggle; the enmity between the woman and the child, and the serpent is portrayed with the triumph of the Child over the forces of evil. The Mother of Jesus is a sign of the Church, or the reality of the Church is expressed in her. The Church in this passage is totally connected to the person of Mary. The woman flees into the desert after the Child is taken to heaven. This is the

---

[4] Feuillet, pp. 17-18.

Church militant that will be protected by God and fed by God as God fed His people in the wilderness. The Church in Revelation 12 is entirely bound to the image of Mary. And as Mary gave birth to Jesus, the Church too, which exists in her image, has children—and we are told that the Devil (who cannot ultimately destroy the Church as a whole) makes war on the rest of her offspring (Revelation 12:17).

The Woman who gives birth in Revelation 12 is Mary. Here we see St. John's theology of the pains of child birth: "When a woman is giving birth she grieves because her *hour* has come, but when she bears a child she no longer remembers her suffering out of joy that a man has come into the world" (John 16:21)— the *hour* of pain is Mary's participation in the Passion of her Son. From the cross Jesus proclaims that Mary is the "Mother of all the living" as John the Beloved Disciple, who represents the faithful of the Church, is her son.

The Church as Bride

Mary in *The Passion* is a sign of the Church. The Church is the covenantal partner of Christ in the accomplishment of redemption. There is at least a hint in the Gibson film that Mary, standing as a sign of the Church, is also a sign of the Church as the Bride of Christ. Mary approaches Jesus on the cross with the words: "Flesh of my flesh." These are the same words spoken by Adam to Eve in the beginning: "Bone of my bones. Flesh of my flesh" (Genesis 2:23). These words carry with them a New Eve theme. In the beginning, Eve was from Adam. Now, as a fulfillment of the Proto Gospel, the New Adam is from the New Eve.

Mary kisses the bleeding feet of Jesus. When Mary pulls away from Him we see the blood of Christ on her lips. It is a moving and startling scene. Russell Hittinger and Elizabeth Lev in their very insightful film review (*First Things*, March 2004) state that in this image Mary is "the bride inebriated with the matrimonial wine." The bridal Church does in fact drink the real Blood of Christ. In this drinking, the covenant is sealed in a love that would die for Christ in response to His love.

At the end of the film the dead and sacrificed Christ is laid in Mary's lap. The blood of Christ is still on her lips. This blood is almost a permanent mark—a red badge of Mary's complete union with her Son. Even though Mary kissed Jesus several moments before, the blood remains. Mary has not erased the sign of her love, unlike Judas who sought to erase the kiss of his betrayal. His kiss drove him out from the company of men. But at the foot of the cross the company of men—that even includes converted Romans—is gathered around the Mother of Jesus. The Mother of Sorrows holds out her hand.

In a gesture of openness, Mary displays her Son's blood-marked body. The viewer is invited in.

Chapter Three

THEMES OF THE INCARNATION

"THE SCREEN WENT BLACK. The torture of Christ had gone on for most of two hours. The resurrection lasted five seconds. If you turned your head you missed it. As I left the theater I could not suppress the thought, 'Such a bloody religion. I wish I were a Buddhist.'"[1]

The Passion of the Christ is a film dominated by violence. The above comment expresses well the desire of many viewers of *The Passion* who wished they could have been spared its horrific violence. After its debut on Ash Wednesday 2004, the violence in the movie became at least as controversial as Gibson's portrayal of the Jews. The violence in *The Passion* is shocking. Consider the reaction of Roger Ebert, the veteran film critic for the *Chicago Sun-Times*. He stated: "This is the most violent film I have ever seen."[2] Keep in mind, this is a man who has watched and studied some of the most violent films ever made. Many film critics believe, and Ebert is among them, that if this were not a religious film, *The Passion* would undoubtedly have received an NC-17 rating.

Any movie that depicts a crucifixion will be violent. Cer-

---

[1] John Zmirak, "The Unbearable Reality of Love: The Passion of the Christ," in Godspy, Faith at the Edge, www.godspy.com, March 5, 2004.

[2] Roger Ebert, "The Passion of the Christ," *Chicago Sun-Times*, February 24, 2004.

tainly, every movie on the life of Christ has its measure of violence. However, the violence of *The Passion* is very different. The word "passion" comes from the Latin. It means "to endure," or "to undergo." The violence of this movie and, just as importantly, the way the movie is filmed, intends to draw the viewer into the reality of suffering. Christ undergoes the Passion, and the audience, whether believers or not, undergo it with Him.

As we will discuss at greater length in Chapter Five, Gibson drew extensively from the visions of Anne Catherine Emmerich's *The Dolorous Passion of Our Lord Jesus Christ*. While Gibson's movie is not for the faint of heart, neither is Emmerich's book. This is a very violent book. Emmerich had visions of Jesus tortured in the most unimaginable kinds of ways. Her visions are saturated with atrocious physical and psychological sufferings of Christ. Here is Emmerich' description of the nailing of Jesus' hands to the cross:

> Then seizing his right arm they dragged it to the hole prepared for the nail, and having tied it down with a cord, one of them knelt upon his sacred chest, a second held his hand flat, and a third, taking a long, thick nail, pressed it on the open palm of that adorable hand... and with a great iron hammer drove it through the flesh, and far into the wood of the cross. Our Lord uttered one deep, but suppressed groan and his blood gushed forth and sprinkled the arms of the archers.... When the executioners had nailed the right hand of our Lord, they perceived that his left hand did not reach the hole they had bored to receive the nail, therefore they tied ropes to his left arm, and having steadied their feet against the cross, pulled the left hand violently until it reached the place prepared for it. This dreadful process caused our Lord indescribable agony, his breast heaved and his legs contracted.

They again knelt upon him, tied down his arms, and drove the second nail into his left hand; his blood flowed afresh, and his feeble groans were once more heard between the blows of the hammer, but nothing could move the hard-hearted executioners to the slightest pity.[3]

The pre-drilled holes in the cross, the stretching of Jesus' arm to make it reach, the blood from the wounds flowing and gushing forth—are Emmerich's images that Gibson incorporated into his film. Gibson may also have borrowed from the Fifteen Meditations of St. Bridget of Sweden, a 14th century mystic. In the 3rd and 4th Meditations St. Bridget describes Jesus' arms being cruelly stretched to fit the cross, dislocating his bones. She also describes Jesus as being entirely covered with wounds. Venerable Mary of Agreda, a 17th century Spanish nun, also sees Christ's limbs stretched and dislocated in her work *The Mystical City of God*.

In both Emmerich's and Gibson's account of the Passion, from the moment of His arrest until His death, Jesus is the victim of unrelieved abuse and cruelties. The violence serves this purpose: it is the portal by which we enter into the truth of the redemption wrought by Christ. *The Passion* is not a movie that is simply intended to *show* the Christian story. Gibson wishes to draw the viewer into the *meaning* of it. He wishes to provoke deep reaction to who Jesus is and what He has done. Of the film Gibson himself stated:

There is a classical Greek word which best defines what "truth" guided my work, and that of everyone else involved with the project: *aletheia*. It simply

---

[3] Anne Catherine Emmerich, *The Dolorous Passion of Our Lord Jesus Christ*, TAN Books, Rockford, IL, 1983, pp. 270-271.

means "unforgetting" (derived from *lethe*—water, from Homer's River Lethe that caused unforgetfulness). It has unfortunately become part of the ritual of our modern secular existence to forget. The film, in this sense, is not meant as an historical documentary nor does it claim to have assembled all the facts. But it does enumerate those described in relevant Holy Scripture. It is not represcntative nor merely expressive. I think of it as contemplative in the sense that one is compelled to remember (unforget) in a spiritual way which cannot be articulated, only experienced.[4]

The images of extreme violence cause the viewer of Gibson's movie to indeed—not forget.

The Theology of Violence

A painting of Jesus as the Man of Sorrows, probably rendered in the first half of the 20th century, was made into a holy card. I have seen this card many times. Jesus is standing up, His hands bound by heavy ropes; He wears a cloak over His shoulders and a piercing crown of thorns upon His head. The card is striking and awful to look at. Christ's body is filled from top to bottom with horrid, open, gaping, bloody wounds. Whole sections of His skin have been flayed off from the scourging. Rivulets of blood pour from these wounds, down His face, His shoulders, His chest, His arms, His legs. When the beaten Christ stands before the crowd in Gibson's film He looks very much like the Christ of this holy card. The graphic and up-close realism of

---

4   Mel Gibson, the "Foreword" in *The Passion* (Photography from the movie, *The Passion of the Christ*), TAN Books, Rockford, IL, 2004.

Christ's physical sufferings affirms the Incarnation of Christ. The Gibson film takes the Incarnation of Christ very seriously: "The Word became flesh and dwelt among us" (John 1:14). This movie is filled with the flesh and blood of Christ. This is the *sarx* (flesh) of the fallen human race, flesh vulnerable and weak—flesh that can suffer, be abused, become sick and die. This is the flesh that Christ took on. He is truly one of us. There is no gnostic, immaterial Christ here. There are no Buddhist escapes from the truth of this material world. *The Passion* will not allow the viewer to escape the prime religious fact of Christianity—that God indeed became a true man. The body of Christ often fills the entire screen. Russell Hittinger and Elizabeth Lev comment on this aspect of the film. They observe that in Zeffirelli's movie, for example, like a Ghirlandaio painting, "the figures occupy only half the canvas."

> By contrast Gibson's figures are in the style of Michelangelo, filling the screen, looming over us, threatening to enter our space. It is unnerving art. When the Roman soldiers call out *"vertere crucem"* the audience tenses. The soldiers lift the cross, prop it on its side for an agonizing moment, and then let it fall over towards us. As it crashes to the ground, an audible gasp sounds in the theater. The viewer is denied the detachment of looking through a window into a faraway world and is drawn into the scenes as a humble, perhaps hapless, participant.... Gibson's disturbing technique of filling the screen with Jesus' body, almost allowing him to tumble into our laps, is contained only by the fact that Mary constantly touches, holds, and comforts the corpus.[5]

---

[5] Russell Hittinger and Elizabeth Lev, "Gibson's *Passion*," *First Things*, No. 141, March 2004.

Occasionally the bloody and bruised face of Jesus occupies the whole screen. We are forced to look at Him as He looks at us. The viewer is confronted by the reality of the God-Man. Often the viewer sees the Passion from Christ's own view of reality.[6] Nothing else but the incarnate Son in the offering of His life for the world matters. When His countenance takes up the whole cinematic space, Jesus is meant to take up the whole spiritual space of the viewer. Some may allow Him in, some, not ready for Him, will be repulsed and flee.

When God becomes Man, history cannot escape Him. Jesus fills time, fills history with Himself. The meaning of history is found in Jesus and the reality of the Incarnation requires a decision. Christ will not be explained away. A reviewer for *New York Press* observed that Gibson "wants to produce images of pain so graphic, intense and unrelenting that they obliterate euphemisms."[7] Complete physical suffering is the metaphor for complete and perfect love. Moreover, the extent of the physical suffering presented in the film is a metaphor for the sins of man that the Son of Man must carry. A well-known author, Garry Wills, who hated the movie, titled his review of the film, "God in the Hands of Angry Sinners."[8] He accused the film of presenting God the Father as bloodthirsty and punishing. The title of his review—a parody of Jonathan Edwards' sermon title, "Sinners in the Hands of an Angry God"—is meant as a criticism of

---

[6] For example, several times the scourging is seen through the eyes of Christ. From His view we see the blood-splattered feet of the soldiers, the upside-down world as Jesus is dragged away (a metaphor perhaps for a world that is spiritually upside-down—the world made by God can't see Him and rejects Him). On the path to Calvary we see the swirling crowd through Jesus' eyes. The flashback of Christ's triumphant entry into Jerusalem is photographed from His view as we see the head and neck of the donkey as Christ is riding it.

[7] Matt Zoller Seitz, "Red-State Deicide: Crucifixion as Bloodbath, Christ as Action Hero," *New York Press*, Vol. 17, Iss. 8, February 26, 2004.

[8] Garry Wills, "God in the Hands of Angry Sinners," *New York Times Review of Books*, Vol. 51, No. 6, April 8, 2004.

what he perceives to be Gibson's Jonathan Edwards-like hell-fire, negative and pessimistic theology. Wills' title is, however, quite ironic. The Jesus of the Gibson film is literally "God in the Hands of Angry Sinners." This is what angry sinners actually do to God when they get hold of Him. It is the love of Christ for these angry, ungrateful sinners that motivates Him to endure the Passion. This is Gibson's point. The Incarnation is real. Sin is real. But the love of Christ is more real than the most horrible sins of men. In one of Emmerich's visions she sees the Devil try to tempt Christ away from the Passion by burdening Him with the reality that, despite His great suffering, many would be ungrateful. Because of His love for people, Christ endures the Passion without a guarantee of gratitude from the human race.

Like the holy card I spoke of earlier, the Christ of *The Passion* endures a physical suffering that literally covers the entirety of His flesh. No part of His flesh is spared. Every exposed area of His body bears an open wound. Most of these wounds are the result of the scourging at the pillar. The viewer watches the beating, first with rods, then with cat-o'-nine-tails in the minutest detail of flesh being flayed off the body of Christ by cruel, mocking Roman goons. Each stroke they inflict is either seen or heard by the audience. Blood is splashed everywhere. Even Christ's tormentors notice they are sprinkled with it. The scene lasts several minutes. By the end of it Jesus is a gaping wound from the top of His head to His feet. The audience is shocked to see Christ's whole body covered by wounds. There is not a space left on His body unaffected by the Passion. The incarnate God enters fully into the human condition. No part of His earthly existence is held back or spared. Moreover, there is no part of the God-Man that is unaffected by the sins of the human race. He really bears the sins of men. The Roman soldiers take immense pleasure in causing Christ pain. Their glee is a theological metaphor. Their satisfaction in causing pain is a commentary on sin and the desire of the human race to indulge its passions contrary to the will of God. In short, the Roman soldiers stand-in for all people.

While the violence of the Gibson film is guided by realism, there is something very unreal about the extreme cruelties Christ endures. Some film critics have remarked, about the scourging and other beatings Christ is subject to, that no human being could have endured such abuse and still be alive for a crucifixion. "Indeed it is doubtful any human being could remain conscious for his own execution were he to endure the level of physical abuse graphically depicted here."[9] This human being, however, is able to absorb cruelties no ordinary person could endure. This, too, is a theological point. The Passion is not endured by an ordinary man. This man takes more, suffers more, endures more because this is the God-Man. Even the Roman soldiers are amazed that Jesus rises to His feet after the caning. They probably never saw that before! The excessive violence of this movie points to the divine nature of the victim. It illustrates Jesus' divinity. Furthermore, the violence of the film is shocking simply because of who is the subject of it. One movie critic remarked: "If you watch a tough action hero like Harrison Ford take a punch in the face, it might seem moderately violent. But if you watch a peaceful figure like Jesus Christ take a black-eye the violence level seems to be much higher."[10] I was seriously unsettled when I watched *The Passion* for the first time and saw Jesus repeatedly punched in the face by the Temple guards. It was not simply that this was a gentle man being beaten. The shock operates on a different level. As a believer I identified the character played by Jim Caviezel as my Lord and my God. Everyone knows Jesus suffered horribly, but I was not prepared to

---

[9] Kirk Honeycutt, "The Passion of the Christ," www.thehollywoodreporter.com, February 23, 2004.

[10] Audrey Rock, "The Passion of the Christ," in "Reel Talk," Transcript-Bulletin, February 27, 2004.

see Jesus treated with such absolute rank disrespect by His tormentors. It was as if some artistic boundary had been crossed—
even a taboo broken—to observe Christ so horrifically mistreated.

Catholic screenwriter Barbara Nicolosi lamented that some
will stay away from *The Passion* including many devout Christians, because of the film's violent content. In her article "'Good'
Screen Violence" she admits, "The images of violence in *The
Passion* are hard to watch. They are truly disturbing on a level
in which I have never been disturbed by a movie before."[11] She
explains however, that while she has never been able to purge
from her mind the terrible torture scenes in films like *Romero,
The English Patient* and *The Fixer*:

> ... yet those films amount to powerful indictments of
> real evils, in the civil war in El Salvador, the Nazis and
> the Mob. These are evils that caused immeasurable
> human suffering. If others had to live it, through no
> fault of their own, isn't there something just in me
> having to watch it, especially from the relatively easy
> life I live, through no particular merit of my own....
> Being disturbed out of complacency and into a soli-
> darity with others' suffering is a good thing.

Nicolosi remarks that the great Catholic writer Flannery
O'Connor defended the harshness of her work by noting wryly,
"I have found that violence uniquely opens my characters to the
truth. The truth is only something we can return to at great cost."
Nicolosi very insightfully comments that the violence of *The
Passion* establishes "a new benchmark for cinema." Not because
it is the most violent film ever made, but "by connecting vio-
lence to its source as a spiritual sickness. Spurred on by Satan,

---

[11] Barbara Nicolosi, "'Good' Screen Violence," *St. Austin Review*, Vol. 4, No. 2,
March/April 2004.

man does violence as an act of hatred against God."[12] Thus this is how Christ looks when God is in the hands of angry sinners.

The Blood of *The Passion*

In the Offertory of the Roman Catholic Eucharistic liturgy the bread and wine, that are transubstantiated into the Body and Blood of Christ, are offered by the priest separately. This is a sign of the death of Christ. Blood is separated from the body in a violent death. If there is one thing you can say about *The Passion of the Christ*, it is that a great deal of Christ's blood is separated from His body. Blood sprays, splatters, spurts, drips, trickles down, collects in pools, smears, clings to garments, clings to hair and literally gushes forth. One reviewer stated that, "Blood becomes a distinctive force in the movie, an element, a character. *The Passion* isn't just a gruesome movie, but a ritual that exalts the blood of Jesus because the release of this blood released humanity from sin."[13]

In the faith of the ancient Hebrew people, blood sacrifice was central to the worship of God. Animals were sacrificed in thanksgiving rituals, to seal covenants and in atonement for sin. Beginning with Abel, who offered an unblemished lamb to God, and who, as a type of Christ, met a violent death, these blood sacrifices fill the whole Old Testament. When God made a covenant with Abraham, He told Abraham to kill various kinds of animals by cutting them in two. Abraham laid each half of their carcasses on the ground. "Now when the sun had set, a smoking brazier and a fiery torch passed between the pieces. On that day the Lord made a covenant with Abraham" (Genesis 15:17-18). God Himself passed through the sacrificed animals, sealing the covenant with His presence.

---

[12] Ibid.

[13] Richard Alleva, "Torturous," *Commonweal*, Vol. 131, No. 5, March 12, 2004.

Blood sacrifice spares the Jews from the plague of the death of the firstborn that God visited upon the Egyptians. Exodus (12:5-13) records the Passover sacrifice:

> The lamb must be a year-old male and without blemish. You may take it from either the sheep or the goats. You shall keep it until the fourteenth day of the month and then, with the whole assembly of Israel present, it shall be slaughtered during the evening twilight. They shall take some of its blood and apply it to the two doorposts and the lintel of every house in which they partake of the lamb.... It is the Passover of the Lord. For on this same night I will go through Egypt, striking down every firstborn of the land, both man and beast, and executing judgment on all the gods of Egypt—I, the Lord! But the blood will mark the houses where you are. Seeing the blood, I will pass over you; thus when I strike the land of Egypt, no destructive blow will come upon you.

The Passover theme of the movie is expressed in the dialogue between the two Marys. When these characters first appear in the film Mary, the mother of Jesus asks, "Why is this night different from every other night?" Mary Magdalen responds, "Because once we were slaves and now we are free." Any Jew would recognize these words as part of the Passover Seder ritual—words the youngest says to the oldest. In the death of Christ, everything that the Passover prefigured is fulfilled.

The covenant between God and the Jews is ratified by blood sacrifice as described in the Book of Exodus (24:3-8):

> When Moses came to the people and related all the words and ordinances of the Lord, they all answered with one voice, "We shall do everything that the Lord has told us."

Moses... then erected at the foot of the mountain an altar and twelve pillars for the twelve tribes of Israel.

Then having sent certain young men of the Israelites to offer holocausts and sacrifice young bulls as peace offerings to the Lord, Moses took half of the blood and put it in large bowls; the other half he splashed on the altar. Taking the book of the covenant he read it aloud to the people, who answered, "All that the Lord has said, we will heed and do." Then he took the blood and sprinkled it on the people saying, "This is the blood of the covenant which the Lord has made with you in accordance with all these words of his."

In Judaism the blood of a living creature was sacred. The Book of Leviticus teaches that the Jews are prohibited from consuming the blood of a sacrificed animal or wasting it. "I will set myself against that one who partakes of blood and will cut him off from among his people. Since the life of a living body is in its blood, I have made you put it on the altar, so that atonement may thereby be made for your own lives, because it is the blood, as the seat of life, that makes atonement" (Leviticus 17:10-11).

The blood poured out of a sacrificed animal was a sign of worship—the life of a living creature that, once poured out, cannot be taken back. It was a symbol of the human being's own consecration to God. Notice, it is by the pouring out of the animal's blood and its consecration to God that atonement for sin is achieved.

The Christian religion is based on the blood sacrifice of Christ, the Lamb of God whose death, in fulfillment of the Old Testament, takes away the sins of the world. Numerous passages in the New Testament speak of the salvific nature of Christ's blood. Let us consider a few of them. St. Paul tells the leaders of the church of Ephesus: "Shepherd the church of God which he has acquired at the price of [Christ's] own blood" (Acts 20:28). In Romans Paul teaches, "Through [Christ's] blood, God made him the means of expiation for all who believe" (Romans 3:25). Later in the same letter Paul states, "Now that we have been justified by [Christ's] blood, it is all the more certain that we shall be saved by him from God's wrath" (Romans 5:9). "It pleased God to make absolute fullness reside in him and, by means of him, to reconcile everything in his person... making peace through the blood... of his cross" (Colossians 1:20). This Pauline theme is also found in Ephesians 1:7 and 2:13.

The doctrine of atonement accomplished in the blood of Christ is central to the Letter to the Hebrews. In this letter Christ is the great and definitive high priest who will offer Himself as the final offering for sin. And the offering is only made through the shedding of His blood.

> He entered not with the blood of goats and calves, but with his own blood, and achieved eternal redemption. For if the blood of goats and bulls and the sprinkling of a heifer's ashes can sanctify those who are defiled so that their flesh is cleansed, how much more will the blood of Christ... cleanse our consciences from dead works to worship the living God....
>
> Hence, not even the first covenant was inaugurated without blood. When Moses read all the commandments of the law to the people, he took the blood of goats and calves... and sprinkled the books and all the people, saying, "This is the blood of the covenant which God has enjoined upon you." He also sprinkled the tabernacle and all the vessels of worship with blood.
>
> According to the law, almost everything is purified by blood, and without the shedding of blood there is no forgiveness (Hebrews 9:12-14, 18-22).

The Johannine tradition also emphasizes that salvation is accomplished in the blood of Christ. He identifies Jesus as the Lamb of God (John 1:29)—as Christ is the true Passover sacrifice acceptable to the Father. The doctrine is affirmed by John's Eucharistic theology: "If you do not eat the flesh of the Son of Man and drink his blood you have no life in you" (John 6:53). Many passages in the Book of Revelation proclaim that salvation is through the blood of Christ. In keeping with the Proto Gospel, the Devil is overcome by "the blood of the Lamb" (Revelation 12:11). In a striking passage, Jesus the Lord of Lords wears "a cloak that had been dipped in blood" (19:13).

In *The Passion* Jesus indeed overcomes the Devil by the pouring out of His blood. Moreover, as His whole body is covered by the wounds of His Passion, Christ literally wears a cloak of blood. On the feast days of martyrs a priest's liturgical vestments are red. Jesus, in the film, does not simply wear a symbolic color of blood. He wears blood. He is dressed in blood because He is the true priest and the true sacrifice. His blood, by which the world shall be saved, is His true garment. Soaked with blood, carrying His cross, Jesus tells Mary, "See, Mother, I make all things new." This line, adapted from Revelation 21:5, is uttered about half way through the movie and indeed it is the center, the key to the Gibson film. By His blood Christ makes all things new.

The Linen Cloths

After Jesus is scourged at the pillar, Mary His mother and Mary Magdalen get down on their hands and knees and mop up the blood of Christ that has collected in pools on the pavement. It is one of the most unexpected and engaging scenes of the movie. The scene is taken directly from the visions of Emmerich. Her description of the scourging is told with much feeling and pathos. It is also very violent and very bloody. Emmerich describes Christ as "bathed in His own blood." And "The body of our Lord was perfectly torn to shreds—it was but one wound." This is the way Christ looks in the film. Emmerich also describes the Roman soldiers in great detail and states that "the soldiers resembled wild beasts or demons, and appeared to be half drunk." Their drunken condition is hinted at in the movie. Just prior to the scourging we see a few of them drinking and laughing loudly. They also drink, are raucous and appear partly inebriated on the Via Dolorosa. This is especially the case when they mock Simon of Cyrene when he protests their brutal treatment of Christ.

Mary and Mary Magdalen wipe up the blood of Jesus with linen cloths given to them by a brokenhearted Claudia—the wife of Pontius Pilate. Pilate's wife is mentioned in the Gospel of Matthew in a short but most intriguing passage: "While [Pilate] was still presiding on the bench, his wife sent him a message, 'Do not interfere in the case of that holy man. I had a dream about him today which has greatly upset me'" (Matthew 27:19). In *The Passion* Claudia Procles, the traditional name given to Pilate's wife, influences him to seek a way to spare Jesus' life. When we first see her, she is in bed, the nightmare already upon her. During the scourging, Pilate's wife very humbly—even meekly—approaches Mary and Mary Magdalen who are weeping. Claudia looks at them and holds out the linen cloths to Mary, almost bowing her head as she does so. Mary and the Magdalen are enormously moved by this unexpected gesture of kindness from a Gentile woman—the wife of the very man responsible for the beating that Christ endures. Once the linens are handed over, Claudia, nearly in tears, quickly vanishes.

Claudia and Mary are brought together by Christ. Claudia, while she has a formal allegiance to Pilate and is publicly defined by her Roman duties as Pilate's wife, is a closet Christian. She is restricted in her discipleship socially, culturally and even politically. Unlike Mary and the Magdalen, Claudia is not able to follow Christ. The audience feels the pain of her restrictions and feels her humiliation that her husband is causing the pain of a man she knows to be holy—and thus pain to His mother. This scene spiritually fulfills the words that Mary Magdalen spoke to Mary earlier in the film: "Once we were slaves, but now we are free." They are free. Claudia is not.

Emmerich speculates that Claudia intends the cloths to be used to bind Christ's wounds. After all, even in the movie, Pilate intends to release Jesus after the beating.

The Themes of the Eucharist

The beating at the pillar is halted and Jesus, unable to walk, is dragged away. The camera focuses on the now vacant and silent courtyard and the finally motionless torture instruments, dripping blood. Mary gets down on her knees, takes one of the linens and carefully begins to wipe up Jesus' blood that has pooled on the pavement. Mary Magdalen removes her veil and does the same. This action is a very important theological statement. First, the blood of Christ is precious. In keeping with the Old Testament theology of blood and sacrifice, it is not to be wasted. This is no ordinary blood, as if the blood of any man were ordinary. But this is the blood by which the world is saved. Moreover and just as importantly, the scene is filled with a deep Eucharistic theme. A commentator on this film explains:

> [The] blood that is splattered all over the scourgers at the Pillar, is the blood we drink on the altar. We say in earnest, what the mob said in unconscious irony: "May his blood be on us and on our children." … Since Gibson is a Catholic, he has no trouble identifying the blood on the floor of the guardroom and the blood in the chalice…. Mary blots up the blood of Christ with

towels just as a Catholic would blot the spilled Precious Blood with a purificator. It's all one for Gibson because it's all one for any Catholic who knows his faith.[14]

This is the first of several Eucharistic images in the Gibson film. The next image is much subtler. The sacrificial death of Jesus begins when Pilate, making a great show of it, has a basin of water brought forth and washes his hands declaring to the crowd, "I am innocent of this man's blood." The film cuts to the Last Supper. A basin has been set before Jesus and He washes His hands. Pilate washes his hands in a vain attempt to disavow his part in Christ's death. Christ washes His hands in preparation for the Eucharist that signifies His death.

The most overt Eucharistic statement of the film occurs when Jesus is on Calvary. Again the film returns to the Last Supper. Warm bread covered in cloth is brought to the table and Jesus unwraps it. The film quickly cuts back to Calvary. Roman soldiers tear off Christ's clothes "unwrapping" His torn and bloody flesh. As Nicolosi explains: "The scene of the stripping of Christ on Calvary... is interrupted by a scene of Christ at the Last Supper, unwrapping the bread for the Passover meal. The association of the two rituals is powerful and haunting: the body of a man being readied for death, a loaf of bread being readied for sacrifice."[15]

Through images and cinematic technique Gibson teaches that the Eucharistic Bread is truly the Body of Christ. This is emphasized later when we are again taken from Calvary to the Last Supper and Jesus pronounces the words that institute the Eucharist: "Take and eat, this is my body which shall be given

---

[14] Mark Shea, one of four contributors to the book, *A Guide to The Passion, 100 Questions About The Passion of the Christ*, Ascension Press and Catholic Exchange, 2004. The above quote is from Mark Shea's Web site: www.Mark-Shea.com

[15] Nicolosi, "'Good' Screen Violence."

up for you." He elevates the bread in a liturgical gesture. In the next scene Christ is on the cross being lifted up. The camera focuses on John who looks at the cross with an expression of amazement. He has penetrated the mystery of the Passover meal. Indeed, it was John who brought the wrapped Passover bread to the table. Now he fully understands the meaning of this Bread. As this character has made the connection between the Eucharistic Bread and Christ on the cross, so too the audience is led to make this connection. Not only are the Eucharistic Bread and the Crucified Body of Christ the same reality, but these images demonstrate that the Eucharist is the representation of the sacrifice of Christ. Indeed, when Jesus elevates the bread, and later the cup, these are the liturgical gestures of the Catholic Mass.

Again we are taken from Calvary to the Last Supper. Christ lifts the chalice of wine and says: "This is my blood, the blood of the Covenant to be poured out on behalf of the many so that sins may be forgiven. Do this in memory of me." The film turns back to Christ on the cross, blood dripping from His hand and down His arm. Again John looks at Jesus with an expression of absolute astonishment.

The words over the cup are a combination from the Gospels of Matthew and Luke. They are the same words of consecration Catholic priests pronounce at Mass. When Mary, John and Mary Magdalen arrive at Calvary they immediately kneel upon the ground. They are the only characters present at the crucifixion who do kneel. Kneeling is a gesture of worship. They are present at the definitive sacrifice worthy of God and are prepared to enter into its mystery. It is because of the kneeling posture that Mary Magdalen is in a privileged position to see a miracle. The Roman soldiers turn the cross over on its side and allow it to fall over with Christ hung upon it. One expects Jesus' face to hit the ground with the weight of the cross on top of Him. But Jesus' body, oddly, does not touch the ground. He is suspended above it. The Magdalen alone notices that Jesus is not on the ground. She can see this miracle because, as a disciple, Mary Magdalen has placed herself in a prostrate, humble position—the position of Christ Himself.

"Flesh of my flesh." These are the words Christ's mother declares to her Son as she stands before the cross. She kisses His feet and His blood is upon her lips. Mary drinks from the original sacramental fount. But the body on the cross, the blood that He sheds has come from her. The Body and Blood of Jesus have a Marian character. Mary is not only spiritually connected to her Son. They are bound together by flesh. As Christ is from her— the Eucharist too is from her. It is through the flesh that came from Mary that salvation is accomplished.

The Shower of Water and Blood

After Christ dies on the cross, the viewer of the film sees the crucifixion as if from God's point of view—from above. It is an odd and unexpected perspective. Not only is it an aerial view, but we look upon the Passion through God's tear. From all sides of the screen a water droplet forms and the camera follows its gradual descent to the ground. Upon its landing, God's tear quakes the earth. The earth shakes, Pilate's house trembles and the Temple is violently rent. The soldiers on Calvary are tossed into panic, fear and confusion. Due to the storm the death of the criminals needs to be hastened and the soldiers, as recorded in John's Gospel, hastily break the legs of the two thieves. Cassius takes up a large hammer to break Jesus' legs but as he approaches the cross he is thrown back by the quaking earth. He cries out above the noise of the storm that Jesus is already dead. Abenader tosses Cassius a lance and tells him to make sure.

Cassius takes the lance. He looks at Mary in a moment of hesitation. He then quickly approaches the cross and thrusts the

49

spear deeply into the side of Christ. Christians are well acquainted with this scene in John's Gospel (19:31-37):

> Since it was the Preparation Day the Jews did not want to have the bodies left on the cross during the Sabbath, for that Sabbath was a solemn feast day. They asked Pilate that the legs be broken and the bodies be taken away. Accordingly, the soldiers came and broke the legs of the men crucified with Jesus, first of the one, then of the other. When they came to Jesus and saw that he was already dead, they did not break his legs. One of the soldiers thrust a lance into his side, and immediately blood and water flowed out.
>
> (This testimony has been given by an eyewitness and his testimony is true. He tells what he knows is true so that you may believe.) These events took place for the fulfillment of Scripture: "Break none of his bones."
>
> There is still another Scripture passage which says: "They shall look on him whom they have pierced."

It is traditionally believed that the eyewitness is the apostle John himself. In any case, the author of the Gospel emphasizes the fact that blood and water poured out of the wound in Christ's side upon His being pierced with the lance. The pouring out of the blood and water is important to him. He dwells on it, highlights it and emphasizes its historicity. Indeed, his testimony concerning the blood and water is meant to arouse faith. The blood and water are described as having "flowed" out. The Greek word simply means "came out."

When I saw the movie for the first time, familiar as I am with the Gospel passage, I expected, of course, that blood and water would come from Christ's side. I expected a trickle. What comes from His side is no trickle. Instead we have the final blood-letting of Christ. A literal shower of blood and water gushes forth. Cassius is hit directly in the face with it. He is completely emotionally overcome—instantly overcome—and drops to his knees as the film's music rises in volume. The blood and water shower him. It continues to spray forth like a never-ending stream. The source of this blood and water seems never to dry up. Cassius, who already was attracted to Mary, is now completely and utterly converted to her Son.

This is the climax of the film. Christ's Passion has accomplished its purpose—conversion, renewal, redemption. The Devil is shown defeated—screaming in the pit of Hell. Theologically the water and blood from the side of Christ are signs of the sacraments of Baptism and Eucharist—the two sacraments upon which the Church is founded. The sheer copiousness of the liquid is a sign of the abundance of the sacramental graces of the Church—a wealth of graces coming from the love of Christ that cannot dry up. The conversion of Cassius is the fitting climax of the Gibson movie. Christ through His Passion brings forth the life-giving waters of Baptism, the life-giving blood of the Eucharist and effects the renewal of the world. From the cross the redemption of sinners is accomplished.

Veronica's Veil

The incarnational theme of *The Passion* finds expression in the scene of Veronica's veil. The character enters the film when we see her on the roof of her house. Her little daughter comes to her weeping and the woman comforts the child. Veronica seems to know that something is happening. She listens intently to the sounds of the crowd on the Via Dolorosa. Jesus has fallen under the weight of the cross. He lies in the street unable to get up. An angry, frenzied crowd attempts to rush at Him. Some throw stones at Him. The Roman soldiers are busy keeping the people away. In the midst of this confusion and hate, Veronica and her daughter suddenly appear. She takes a cup of water from the little girl and approaches Jesus. Veronica enters a scene stirring with chaos and evil but she is calm, serene and walks with a resolute spirit—in complete contrast to the world that is opposed to Christ.

Veronica kneels where Jesus is half sprawled on the ground. He looks at her. She says, "Permit me, my Lord." She takes off her veil and raises it up. Jesus takes it in His hands and presses it to His bleeding face as He breathes a deep gasp of relief. He hands the cloth back to her. She looks at Him with deep sorrow and presses the veil to her lips like a sacred relic. Veronica then takes the cup of water and hands it to Jesus, but abruptly their world of peace is shattered. The hate and brutality of the outer world stomps into the inner world of love. Even the audience is jarred by this violent intrusion. One of the soldiers pushes the cup away, the water splashes out. The moment of kindness is ended as Veronica is bullied and chased away.

Christ gets up and resumes His march to Calvary. Jesus looks at Veronica as He and Simon of Cyrene pass by her while carrying the cross. Jesus and Veronica share a glance for a long moment. Veronica stands on the side of the street holding the holy cloth—the features of Jesus' suffering countenance stamped upon it in blood. The cloth records the suffering of Christ and Veronica stands with her sign in public witness to her love for the condemned man.

This scene is not in Scripture. It is from Catholic spiritual tradition. However, almost every movie about Jesus includes, however briefly, a woman mercifully wiping Christ's face on His way to Calvary. Veronica's wiping the face of Christ is one of the fourteen Stations of the Cross found in nearly every Catholic church. There has been much historical speculation and debate about the existence of this veil. Veronica herself is mentioned in the apocryphal *Acts of Pilate* and is identified as the woman Jesus cured of a flow of blood. According to tradition, Veronica came to Rome—summoned there by Emperor Tiberius who was cured of an illness upon touching the veil. Just prior to her death Veronica gave the veil to Clement I who was pope at the end of the first century A.D. A cloth that bears the imprint of a man's face, very similar in its features to the face on the famous Shroud of Turin, is kept at the monastery in Monoppello, Italy. This 6½ by 9½ inch cloth has, like the Shroud, been the subject of several scientific studies.

Whether this woman actually lived or not, the tradition of Veronica's veil serves a very important theological purpose. The name "Veronica" is a combination of Latin and Greek and means "true image." An image of the face of Christ is possible because He truly did become a man. When God enters history He leaves His imprint upon the material world. When God enters time, His actions, while those of a supernatural person, can be recorded. Indeed, ironically, because of the Incarnation, something of the unfathomable mystery of God can be captured and "frozen" by art. *The Passion* emphasized this fact very well. In the film the real Christ passes by while Veronica holds the captured, static image of this very same living reality. The cloth that she holds in her hand points to Him. His presence is passing, but the image remains. Veronica's replica of Christ is in the background of the scene, while the reality of the suffering Christ is in the foreground. Oddly, however, it is the image of the suffering Christ on the cloth that is, at least momentarily, compelling. The viewer wishes to see it, study it, and ponder it because the true icon attracts. The image draws us to the truth. It draws us to the truth of the suffering God-Man. Veronica's veil is the ultimate icon. In the film it does what any authentic icon is meant to do—deepen faith and contemplation of the eternal mysteries. While the God-Man is risen, the image of His incarnate suffering love remains.

Chapter Four

ACCEPTERS AND REJECTERS

A T THE BEGINNING OF THE PATH to Calvary Jesus is presented with His cross. He doesn't just take it; He doesn't just pick it up because He has to. The Christ of *The Passion* literally embraces it. This gesture is completely unexpected. No other Jesus on film ever actually hugged the cross. This image, of course, serves the movie's theological message—Christ willfully takes on the work of redemption. As Gesmas the "bad" thief is fitted with the crossbeam over his shoulders he mocks Christ, calling Him a fool. According to his world one does not take on suffering, one curses it. This character is the focus of one of the most disturbing and most misunderstood actions of the film. Consistent with the Gospel of Luke, this thief blasphemes Jesus from the cross: "If you're the Messiah, save yourself and us." The good thief, Dismas, rebukes him. He cries out that they are getting what they deserve for their crimes, but Jesus is innocent. A few moments later a large black bird flies to the cross of Gesmas and perches on the beam to the right of his head. The bird's size and color—perched as it is above a completely vulnerable man—portends a kind of awful doom. The thief looks at the bird. With one eye he focuses upon it. Suddenly the bird drives his beak into the eye. The wretched criminal screams in pain as the bird gouges him several times before being mercifully driven off by one of the Roman soldiers. It is a horrifying scene.

Some critics interpret the black bird as God's punishment of the thief for cursing His Son. David Ansen of *Newsweek* saw it this way as well as Philip A. Cunningham of the Center for Christian-Jewish Learning at Boston College. He attributes this action to an unforgiving God who sends a "raven" to "peck out the eye of the presumably ignorant crucifixion victim who has taunted Jesus."[1]

Such critics completely miss the theological meaning of this horrific scene. The black bird is not on the side of God, but on the side of Satan. Earlier in the movie, just as Jesus is brought before Pilate, another bird appears. It is a white bird flying overhead. Jesus looks up at it. He alone takes any notice of it as if the bird, possibly a sign of the Holy Spirit, were sent to strengthen Him. Why should a black bird pluck the eye of the "bad" thief? His eyes, given for seeing, have failed to see. The thief is spiritually blind—he has eyes, but cannot see the identity of the God-Man who hangs next to him. When one uses his sight wrongly one loses it. By refusing to acknowledge Jesus and cursing Him, the thief has placed himself on the side of Satan. Now indeed he is Satan's prey and the bird of Hell may have his way with him. Even after his eye has been gouged, Gesmas continues to taunt Christ. After Jesus cries out, "Eloi, Eloi lama sabachthani?" — "My God, my God, why have You abandoned me?"— Gesmas tries to demoralize Christ by telling Him that He is alone—all have left Him.

The Passion and the Jews

Arguably, the most controversial element of *The Passion* is the way those who reject Christ are depicted, most particularly Caiaphas and other leaders of the Jewish Sanhedrin. Even be-

---

[1] Philip A. Cunningham, "Gibson's *The Passion of the Christ:* A Challenge to Catholic Teaching," Boston College web site, www.bc.edu, February 25, 2004.

fore the film was released, many Jewish and Christian leaders and theologians accused the film of anti-Semitism. Abraham H. Foxman, national director of the Anti-Defamation League, seven months before the film's official debut and without yet seeing the film, expressed serious objections to it. He echoed the concerns of many Jewish leaders who cited the "long history of the Passion story" as "holding the Jewish people responsible for killing Jesus."

According to this interpretation, both the Jews at the time of Jesus and the Jewish people for all time bear a divine curse for the sin of deicide. Throughout nearly 1,900 years of Christian-Jewish history, the charge of deicide has led to hatred and violence against Jews of Europe and America, and various forms of anti-Semitic expression.

Historically, Holy Week (the week leading up to Easter Sunday) was a period when Jews were most vulnerable and when Christians perpetrated some of the worst violence against their Jewish neighbors.[2]

Rabbi Daniel Lapin, who defended *The Passion* against the charge of anti-Semitism, also acknowledged that many Jews protest *The Passion* because "[I]n Europe, anti-Semitic slander frequently resulted in Catholic mobs killing Jews. Our hypersensitivity has a long and painful background of real tragedy."[3]

Film critic Matt Zoller Seitz expressed the concerns of those who do believe the film is unfair to the Jews. He stated that the Romans "are permitted a whole range of reactions—from the goonish guards' chortling sadism to Pilate's spinelessness to the appalled reaction of a young centurion who watches the scourging with tears in his eyes." Except for a few priests, Jesus' dis-

---

[2] Abraham H. Foxman, "Gibson's Passion," Anti-Defamation League web site, www.adl.org, August 4, 2003. This article also appeared in the *New York Sun*, August 4, 2003.

[3] Rabbi Daniel Lapin, "Protesting Gibson's Passion Lacks Moral Legitimacy," Toward Tradition web site, www.towardtradition.org, September 22, 2003.

ciples and His mother, "the Jews are depicted as nearly mono-
lithic in their disdain for Christ and their enjoyment of his suffering."[4]

> Gibson will certainly argue that anti-Semitism is in
> the eye of the beholder—that it is lunacy to suggest
> that just because a few Jews gave up Christ to the
> Romans, then it logically follows that all Jews are col-
> lectively responsible for Christ's death. Such an ar-
> gument would make about as much sense as insisting
> that African Americans bear collective responsibility
> for the murder of Malcolm X, or that Muslims should
> collectively be blamed for 9/11.[5]

Seitz accuses *The Passion* of being "a powder keg of anti-
Semitic imagery":

> Gibson insists that "all humankind was responsible for
> Jesus' death," but the movie implies that some hu-
> mans are more responsible than others. ("It is he who
> delivered me to you who has the greater sin," Jesus
> tells Pilate; if the words of Jesus don't reflect the
> director's viewpoint, I don't know what does.) I hope
> the film's juxtaposition of dusky-skinned, hook-nosed
> Pharisees and images of a bloodied Jesus nailed up on
> a cross won't make bigots feel vindicated, much less
> empowered.[6]

Seitz is not the only commentator who incorrectly inter-
prets the line, "He who handed me over to you has the greater

---

[4] Matt Zoller Seitz, "Red-State Deicide," *New York Press*, Vol. 17, Iss. 8, February
     26, 2004.

[5] Seitz.

[6] Ibid.

sin." John Meacham did so in his cover story for *Newsweek* when he emphatically concluded that "the 'he' in this case refers to Caiaphas."[7] Even Philip Cunningham of Boston College believes Gibson intended the line to refer to Caiaphas. The phrase is found in John's Gospel (19:11) and is not a reference to Caiaphas, but to Judas and there is absolutely no indication in Gibson's film that the person in question is other than Judas. Cunningham accuses Gibson of making it refer to Caiaphas because immediately after Jesus utters the line, Caiaphas says, "If you release him, governor, you are no friend of Caesar." However, Gibson has not manipulated anything here. In John's Gospel the Jews shout, "If you free this man you are no 'Friend of Caesar.' Anyone who makes himself a king becomes Caesar's rival" (John 19:12). Artistically it just makes sense for the chief spokesman for the crowd to have this line.

The Jewish Bad-Guy

Caiaphas, Annas, members of the Sanhedrin and the Jewish witnesses against Christ all look Jewish. A few of them are even "hook-nosed." But if hook-noses were an indication of villainy then Peter the Apostle would be the most villainous of all—as the actor who plays this role has an extremely pronounced hook-nose. One commentator observed:

> In the past, Passion plays sometimes fomented Jew hatred by linking the New Testament persecutors of Jesus with contemporary Jews. These renditions depicted the Temple authorities wearing prayer shawls, phylacteries, side-locks, beards, and hook noses that emphasized their "Jewish" identity in ways modern Europeans would readily recognize.

---

[7] John Meacham, "Who Killed Jesus?" *Newsweek*, February 16, 2004.

Gibson's film pointedly avoids such inflammatory stereotypes. In fact the words "Jew" or "Jewish" seldom, if ever, appear in the subtitles. The high priest and his followers most certainly come across as vicious, self-important, and bloodthirsty, but they seem motivated by pomposity, arrogance and insecurity rather than religious corruption or ethnic curse. The movie also avoids the regrettable tendency of other cinematic treatments of the death of Jesus, in which Judas and the conniving priests of the Temple look swarthy and Semitic, but Jesus and his loyal followers appear all-American, or even Nordic such as the great Swedish actor, Max von Sydow who played Jesus in the 1965's *The Greatest Story Ever Told*. In *The Passion* on the other hand, Gibson emphasizes the Jewish identity of his hero as other characters.[8]

Caiaphas is certainly the "bad-guy" in Gibson's film. He is a one-dimensional character, completely sure of himself and his mission who unrelentingly seeks the crucifixion of Christ. Even when Pilate presents the thoroughly beaten Jesus to the crowd and asks, "What would you have me do with Jesus of Nazareth?" Caiaphas points to Christ and cries out without hesitation, "Crucify him!" His lack of pity is almost shocking. His villainy is matched by Annas, the second spokesman for Christ's death. Many commentators on *The Passion* explain that Caiaphas and the other Jewish leaders are motivated by a desire to maintain power and authority against a rival whose teachings they find threatening and seditious. Roger Ebert stated, "My own feeling is that Gibson's film is not anti-Semitic, but reflects a range of behavior on the part of its Jewish characters, on balance favorably. The Jews who seem to desire Jesus' death are in the priest-

---

[8] Reverend Dr. Gordon Moyes, "The Crucifixion of Mel Gibson," www.wesleymission.org, February 24, 2004.

hood, and have political as well as theological reasons for acting as they do; like today's Catholic bishops who were slow to condemn abusive priests, Protestant TV preachers who confuse religion with politics, or Muslim clerics who are silent on terrorism, they have an investment in their positions and authority."[9]

Regarding the Jews, Mark Shea similarly observed that, "As a Catholic I was moved far more to think of some of my own bishops and their selfish clinging to power than I was to generalities about the International Jew or some sort of theorizing about racial guilt. Caiaphas acts, not as all Jews act, but as all corrupt men act—particularly when they are clinging to power. As the reviewer for TIME [magazine] pointed out, calling criticism of the Sanhedrin 'anti-Semitic' is as dumb as saying, 'Either you are with the Republican Party or you are with the Terrorists.'"[10]

Fidelity to the New Testament

The Passion shows Pontius Pilate as conflicted and complex, and he is afforded a speech that expresses his doubts and fears, while Caiaphas has no doubts and no such speech. Gibson could have deflected a lot of criticism had he at least allowed Caiaphas the one line from Scripture that reveals his reasons for seeking Christ's death. After Jesus raised Lazarus from the dead many Jews began to place their faith in Him:

> Some others, however went to the Pharisees and reported what Jesus had done. The result was that the chief priests and the Pharisees called a meeting of the Sanhedrin. "What are we to do," they said, "with this

---

[9] Roger Ebert, "The Passion of the Christ," *Chicago Sun-Times*, February 24, 2004.

[10] Mark Shea, "Passion Movie Review," Shea's Web site: www.fontfamily.com, March 27, 2004.

man performing all sorts of signs? If we let him go on like this, the whole world will believe in him. Then the Romans will come in and sweep away our sanctuary and our nation." One of their number named Caiaphas, who was high priest that year, addressed them at this point: "You have no understanding whatever! Can you not see that it is better for you to have one man die for the people than to have the whole nation destroyed?" (He did not say this on his own. It was rather as high priest for that year that he prophesied that Jesus would die for the nation—and not for this nation only, but to gather into one all the dispersed children of God.)

From that day onward, there was a plot afoot to kill him (John 11:46-53).

Cunningham accused the film of being unfair to the Jews and provided a very thorough critique of the movie's treatment of them. He argued that Gibson could have arranged the biblical material differently and provided a balanced and fair presentation of the Jews. For instance: "Jesus is arrested by Temple guards and Roman soldiers" (John 18:3), or "Jesus was scourged as part of the Roman crucifixion procedure when Pilate ordered his execution" (Mark 15:15 as against John 19:1-8ff).[11]

No matter what choice of texts Gibson could have used, he is faithful to the New Testament when in the film the leaders of the Sanhedrin have Christ arrested, accuse Him of blasphemy for claiming to be the Son of God and, without hesitation, press for His execution. Moreover, also faithful to Scripture, the film shows quite clearly that some members of the Sanhedrin were sympathetic to Christ.

Many defend *The Passion* because it is faithful to Scripture.

---

[11] Cunningham.

Roy Schoeman, a Jewish convert to Catholicism and author of the book *Salvation is From the Jews*, explains that *The Passion* "accepts the Gospel accounts of the death of Jesus at face value, rejecting the demythologizing reinterpretations that have become the pseudo-dogma of the past several decades."[12] As one commentator noted, "It is the Scriptures that implicate the leaders of the Jews in the death of Jesus, not Mel Gibson."

> Gibson insists that "The Passion" is meant to make everyone uncomfortable, not just Jews.... Gibson remains fiercely determined to bring to the screen what he considers the truth of the New Testament. That the Judean priests and the Judean mob played a prominent role in demanding the death of Christ is Christian mainstream understanding. In John's Gospel, his fellow Jews repeatedly attempt to stone Jesus and cry "Crucify him, crucify him" (19:6). In Matthew the Jewish mob howls, "His blood be on us and on our children" (27:5)—an explosive line which Gibson excised in the final version. Authoritative Jewish sources teach that Jesus died at least partly because of decisions taken by his fellow Jews. The very idea that a two-hour movie could generate a new wave of anti-Semitic violence makes no sense. Anyone disposed to hostility towards the Jews already knows the elements of the Gospels that are unflattering to Jews; there's no need for Mel Gibson to remind them.[13]

Jewish film critic Michael Medved also recognized that *The Passion* is true to Christian Scriptures: "In fact all of the most controversial scenes and lines of dialogue stem directly from the

---

[12] Roy Schoeman, "Caught in the Crossfire," *National Review Online*, February 25, 2004.

[13] Moyes.

Gospels, chapter and verse. This means that critics of the movie should inevitably train their fire on Saints Matthew, Mark, Luke and John rather than 'Saint' Mel."[14] Medved rejects the idea that Christians should have to repudiate their own Christian tradition in favor of a Jewish view of what happened to Jesus. Moreover, he argues that it is a mistake for Jewish critics of the film to make an "unbreakable association between today's Jews and the corrupt Roman collaborator Caiaphas, high priest in the Temple at the time of Jesus."

On March 11, 2004 Joaquin Navarro-Valls, the director of the Vatican's press office, in response to Riccardo Di Segni, chief rabbi of Rome, stated that "*The Passion of the Christ* is a cinematic transcription of the Gospels. If it were anti-Semitic, the Gospels would also be so."[15]

When Gibson shows the leaders of the Sanhedrin as resolute, even vicious in their opposition to Jesus and His teaching, the film maker has support from the whole breadth of the New Testament and the history of the first century Church. This discussion must take place with respect for Judaism, but also with honesty. Even if Jesus were not the Messiah and Son of God incarnate, this man wound up enduring one of the most terrible executions any man could suffer.

Jesus did not just happen to be crucified. Such an extreme punishment is the result of real human activity, real decisions— the result of other people willfully seeking the death of a man— the willful decisions of some Romans and some Jews who were personally involved. That is the historical truth. But the theological truth is more important. It is a truth that Gibson has had to articulate against the accusation that *The Passion* is anti-Semitic—namely the doctrine that all people are responsible for

---

[14] Michael Medved, "Falling Into the 'Passion' Pit," *The Jerusalem Post*, February 19, 2004.

[15] Joaquin Navarro-Valls, quoted in Catholic League for Religious and Civil Rights news release, March 12, 2004.

the death of Christ. In the 16th century the Roman Catholic Church's Council of Trent declared that all men share responsibility for the Passion and that Christians are particularly responsible. "In this guilt are involved all those who fall frequently into sin.... This guilt seems more enormous in us than in the Jews since, if they had known it, they would never have crucified the Lord of glory; while we, on the contrary, professing to know him, yet denying him by our actions, seem in some sort to lay violent hands on him."[16]

Gibson himself stated, "This film collectively blames humanity for the death of Jesus. Now there are no exceptions there. All right? I'm the first on the line for culpability. I did it. Christ died for all men for all times."[17] Gibson has made much of the fact that in the film it is his hand that holds the nail that is driven into Jesus' palm.

Within the context of the New Testament, Christ came to His own and yet was ultimately not accepted by them. It is not expected that the pagan world should know and understand Jesus, but the writers of the New Testament are particularly grieved that, on the whole, beginning with the Jewish leaders, the Hebrew people rejected their Messiah. Gibson's movie, in committing to the screen a New Testament drama, reflects this rejection. It is part of the drama of Christ's life and certainly part of the Passion story. All of the Gospels record the constant conflict Jesus had with the Pharisees, the Scribes and the Sadducees. The Jewish leaders complain that He breaks the Sabbath, does not observe the Jewish dietary laws (Mark 7:5, Matthew 15:1-2) and associates with sinners (Matthew 9:11, Luke 5:30). They are scandalized that He forgives sins on His own authority (Matthew 9:3, Mark 2:6) and by His claim to have existed before Abraham (John 8:57-59). The Jewish leaders of-

---

[16] *The Catechism of the Council of Trent*, TAN Books and Publishers, Rockford, IL, 1982, p. 57.

[17] Meacham.

ten try to trip Him up or put Him to the test (Matthew 16:1, 19:3, Mark 8:11, 12:13). He is accused of being possessed by the Devil (Mark 3:22, John 8:48, 52) and accused of blasphemy for His claim to be the divine Son of God (John 10:23). Jesus tells a crowd of Jews at the Temple that they are trying to kill him (John 7:19 also 8:40) and is warned by His disciples not to go back to Jerusalem upon hearing that Lazarus had died because the Jews only recently tried to stone Him there (John 11:8). Jesus complains that, despite the many signs He has performed, the Jews still will not believe (Matthew 11:20-24, Luke 10:13-15). Jesus calls the Pharisees and Scribes "frauds," "whitened sepulchers, beautiful to look at on the outside, but on the inside filled with filth and dead men's bones," "Viper's nest," "Brood of serpents" (Matthew 23:15, 27, 33) and cries out in grief, "O Jerusalem, Jerusalem, murderess of prophets and stoner of those who were sent to you! How often have I yearned to gather your children, as a mother bird gathers her young under her wings, but you refused me" (Matthew 23:37).

Mark's Gospel records that after Jesus cured a man with a withered hand on the Sabbath, He looked around at the Pharisees in anger "for he was deeply grieved that they had closed their minds against him" (Mark 3:5). The passage also states, "When the Pharisees went outside, they immediately began to plot how they might destroy him" (v. 6).

Many of Jesus' parables speak of His rejection (Matthew 21:33-45, 22:1-14, Luke 16:19-31). The Jewish leaders knew that Jesus was referring to them and they sought to arrest Him (Matthew 21:33-45). Jesus, amazed at the great faith of a Roman centurion, used the occasion to foretell that "Many will come from the east and the west and find a place at the banquet in the kingdom of God with Abraham, Isaac and Jacob, while the natural heirs of the kingdom will be driven into the dark. Wailing will be heard there and the grinding of teeth" (Matthew 8:11-12). Jesus even accuses a crowd of His Jewish opponents of having Satan as their father because they refuse to accept that He has come from God (John 8:44).

Perhaps the saddest line in all Scripture is found in the prologue of John's Gospel: "Through him the world was made, yet the world did not know who he was. To his own he came, yet his own did not accept him" (1:10-11).

From the very beginning of its existence the Church experienced sharp opposition from the Sanhedrin as the Jewish leaders tried to suppress the mission of the apostles. This is clearly recorded in the Acts of the Apostles. Paul, who first persecuted the Church, later expressed his terrible grief over the Jews' lack of faith: "I speak the truth in Christ. I do not lie. My conscience bears me witness in the Holy Spirit that there is great grief and constant pain in my heart. Indeed, I could even wish to be separated from Christ for the sake of my brothers, my kinsmen the Israelites" (Romans 9:1-2).

Jesus and Judaism

It is a spiritual tragedy when men and women reject the Gospel after it is lovingly preached to them. It is certainly no less a tragedy that the vast majority of the Jews have not accepted Jesus. This tragedy is reflected in the Gibson film. The movie is not against the Jews, nor does it intend to blame all Jews forever for Christ's death. Nonetheless, *The Passion* does intend to make a theological statement about Judaism and Jesus' relation to Judaism. This movie takes the Jewish rejection of Jesus seriously. From the spiritual point of view the movie thinks it is a problem. Schoeman expressed the dilemma of Christianity and Judaism very well:

> [I]t is precisely because Christianity teaches that Jesus came as the Jewish Messiah to the Jewish people that the religion implies that Judaism is in fundamental

error in its rejection of Jesus as the Messiah. The "Christian" theologians who have taken the lead in attacking the film—many of them leaders in the "Jewish-Christian" dialogue—have generally made their careers by sidestepping this dilemma by asserting either that Jesus was simply a great moral and ethical teacher, a Rabbi among Rabbis, whose later disciples conferred divine status upon him (a view that is by definition non-Christian); or that Jesus introduced Christianity as a way for non-Jews to enter the Jewish covenant but never intended for Jews to become Christian, an interpretation which is contradicted throughout the Gospels. In either case, in their minds, "Gospel Truth" is bunk.

Hence, the attacks against the movie rest on the claim that its literal acceptance of the Gospels makes it unhistorical and anti-Semitic. This supposed anti-Semitism is produced not by the Gospels themselves, but by the false separation of Christianity from Judaism, that is part of the modernist spin.... Our culture pretends that Judaism and Christianity are two separate but equal religions, with equal validity. But that is intrinsically illogical—one or the other must be wrong. They are one and the same faith, separated only by the matter of whether or not Jesus was the Jewish Messiah, and the religious consequences stemming from that fact. Yet mention of this point must be avoided at all costs... for it implies that either Jesus was the Jewish Messiah, and all of today's Jews are mistaken, or that Jesus was not, in which case Christianity is a grotesque and idolatrous error.[18]

---

[18] Schoeman. See also Jewish convert Rosalind Moss, "It Was Sin That Killed Our Savior: Reflections on Mel Gibson's *The Passion of the Christ*," *This Rock* magazine, April 2004.

The Passion of the Christ isn't just a drama in which some characters oppose Christ. The larger spiritual issue concerning Judaism and Jesus is illustrated by a number of scenes and images. The first image occurs during Christ's trial before the Sanhedrin. When Caiaphas accuses Jesus of blasphemy and cries for His death, a single tear forms in Christ's left eye and falls down His swollen and bloody cheek.

It is interesting to note that donkeys appear in the film in three different, but related contexts. We have already discussed the meaning of the dead donkey carcass as it relates to Judas—a sign of his own inner corruption. A flashback appears in the movie of Jesus riding a donkey during His triumphant entry into Jerusalem. The same path where He was welcomed as King is the same path that He now treads on the way to Calvary. Christ rode a living donkey in acceptance, but the dead, rotting donkey cast away and abandoned on the side of the road is the sign of betrayal and rejection. Caiaphas, Annas and other leaders of the Sanhedrin ride donkeys to the execution of Jesus. They are literally connected to an animal that served to present the accepted Jesus but now lies abandoned and decayed upon the roadside next to Christ's betrayer. The Jewish leaders are placed on the side of Judas—on the side of what fails to accept Jesus. At first, the donkey is the vehicle by which goodness is exalted. Now ridden by the Jewish leaders to the death of Jesus, it is the vehicle by which corruption is exalted.

After Jesus dies on the cross, the Temple veil is rent by the violent earthquake. Caiaphas and other members of the Sanhedrin are devastated. In the great upheaval Caiaphas burns his hand in the fire of one of the Temple urns. He looks about himself as the destruction continues. He is filled with great fear and he weeps. Matthew, Mark and Luke record that the veil in the Temple sanctuary was torn in two. Only Matthew's Gospel mentions that an earthquake also took place. The veil in the Temple concealed the Holy of Holies—that place in the Temple that contained the Ark of the Covenant. When Christ dies, salvation is accomplished and the New Covenant poured out in His blood is open to all people—thus the great holy place of God is revealed. Moreover, the veil is torn as a sign that Christ fulfilled the Law and all Old Covenant expectations. The great High Priest has entered in.

However, in the Gibson film it is the Temple itself that is torn apart, including that part of the Temple that contains the Holy of Holies. It is interesting that the building itself is ruptured. Jesus speaks about the Temple building and its destruction:

> As he was making his way out of the Temple area, one of his disciples said to him, "Teacher, look at the huge blocks of stone and the enormous buildings." Jesus said to him, "You see these great buildings? Not one stone shall be left upon another—all will be torn down." While he was seated on the Mount of Olives facing the Temple, Peter, James, John and Andrew began to question him privately. "Tell us, when will this occur? What will be the sign that all this is coming to an end?" (Mark 13:1-4).

The rent Temple in *The Passion* is a sign that "all this is coming to an end." The sacrifice of Christ has made the Temple and its sacrifices and its priesthood no longer necessary. What Caiaphas had hoped to maintain by putting Christ to death is, ironically, now a "thing of the past"—as Christ by His death has "made all things new." What Caiaphas had so desperately and vehemently clung to no longer exists in the form that he had hoped to preserve it. The Gibson film makes this statement: Christianity supercedes Judaism. The future is in the Temple, but it is the Temple of the resurrected Jesus who appears at the end of the film.

Forgiveness and Not a Curse

When Jesus is dying on the cross, Caiaphas approaches Him and taunts Him about destroying the Temple and raising it in three days. Jesus cries out, "Father forgive them for they know not what they do." Caiaphas turns away. The good thief looks at Caiaphas and says, "He prays for you!" The thief does not look at the Roman soldiers or anyone else in the crowd. His words are directed specifically to Caiaphas. Caiaphas looks very uncomfortable that anyone should suggest he needs prayers. Earlier in the film Caiaphas had called down a curse, "Let his blood be on us and on our children" (the actor says the line, but it is not in the subtitles). When Caiaphas taunts Jesus on the cross, Jesus answers him, not with a curse, but with words of forgiveness. As one reviewer of the film observed:

> The film is rich with suggestions, with moving moments that demonstrate how Jesus is indeed the face of a loving God turned toward man.... We see him rescue Mary Magdalen from a crowd of righteous Pharisees—who all too eagerly seek to enforce the Mosaic law by stoning her. Wracked with torture which we share, crushed by mockery, and tempted to despair—He turns to Dismas, the penitent thief, and promises him, "This day you will be with me in my kingdom." And most astonishingly, He turns to the gloating Caiaphas, who taunts him from the foot of the cross..., and looks directly at him as He delivers his final absolution: "Father forgive them, for they know not what they do." This phrase utterly negates Caiaphas' hasty, callous curse, "Let his blood be upon us and upon our children." (...) Jesus refutes him, with divine authority; it is not guilt, but forgiveness, which will pour from the cross and descend upon the ages.[19]

---

[19] Shea.

Herod

Perhaps the one character most overlooked is Herod. Certainly he is on the side of those who do not understand Christ, much less accept Him. He comes into the film as a way for Pilate, at the prompting of Claudia, to avoid condemning Christ to death. The leaders of the Sanhedrin bring Christ to Herod only reluctantly. Herod enters the movie "stage left," hastily donning a wig and accompanied by a male escort. Both are giddy and laughing as if drunk. The audience is immediately struck by Herod's foppish nature. His environment drips with decadence and irresponsibility. Emmerich described Herod as a "luxurious and effeminate prince." *The New York Press* film critic believed Gibson's portrayal of Herod was homophobic as the film "depicts King Herod as a be-wigged, Dom Deluise-style fop lording it over a court full of queens."[20] Such an unequivocal criticism doesn't match the very blurry, equivocal portrayal of Herod in the film. Yes, young men attend Herod, but there are plenty of young decadent women in the court too. The presence of these women makes Herod's sexual orientation uncertain. Perhaps he is bisexual. It's hard to tell. There's only a small hint that perhaps Herod is a homosexual when, embedded in the film's credits, is the phrase, "Herod's boy," followed by the name of the actor who played the part. Regardless of whether Gibson intended Herod to be gay, the very fact that his sexual orientation is a matter for debate is significant.

It should be noted that the portrayal of Herod as effeminate is not new with Gibson. There seems to be a Hollywood tradition of depicting corrupt Jewish and Roman rulers as "limp-wristed." Jay Robinson in the 1954 film *The Robe* interpreted the part of Caligula this way. Robinson also played the same part in *Demetrius and the Gladiators.* Peter Ustinov's Nero in the 1951

---

[20] Seitz.

movie *Quo Vadis* is certainly effeminate, and an effeminate Pontius Pilate, played by Frank Thring appears in the 1959 *Ben Hur*. Thring's effeminate gestures also were evident in his portrayal of Herod in the 1961 *King of Kings*. Pontius Pilate also appears quite "gay" in the 2001, made-for-TV movie *Jesus*. Emperor Commodus, played by Joaquin Phoenix in *Gladiator*, while extremely good-looking, was less than virile and had incestuous feelings for his own sister. "Soft" masculinity seems to be a theatrical metaphor for the corrupt use of power. Interestingly, the directors of these films are not accused of homophobia—though admittedly the effeminate nature of Gibson's Herod is cranked up a few notches.

There is only one other character in *The Passion* whose sexuality is indeterminate—and that is Satan himself. Sexual ambivalence is on the side of evil. Satan sort of looks like a woman, but sometimes acts and sounds like a man; Herod looks like a man, but sort of sounds and acts like a woman. Undefined, confused or decadent sexuality is a sign of what is partial and weak, even dishonest—and in this they are contrary to God's will for human identity. Contrast these characters to Jesus and Mary—fully man, fully woman. As such they are able to take on adult responsibilities and are able to fulfill what it means for them to be the New Adam and the New Eve.

Simon of Cyrene

All three Synoptic Gospels mention Simon the Cyrenean as being "pressed" into service to carry Jesus' cross. Luke says that he was "laid hold of" to carry Christ's cross. The language of the Gospels definitely tells the reader that Simon did not willingly volunteer for the job. Simon of Cyrene is a major character in Gibson's film and through him the viewer is treated to a wonderful theological feast. The character in the film has African features. In *The Greatest Story Ever Told* Sidney Poitier, a well-known black actor, played Simon. Often, Christian art portrays Simon as a black man. This is due to the fact that the ancient town of Cyrene was in North Africa in what is now modern-day Libya. It is conjectured that Simon was an African Jew. Given our contemporary awareness of the injustice of slavery and discrimination, how appropriate it is that a black man is forced into a labor he does not want—a sign of the injustice of forced labor that Africans endured. In this Simon, the black man, suffers with Christ.

In *The Passion* Jesus is crushed with exhaustion on the Via Dolorosa. The Roman soldiers try to get Jesus to continue carrying the cross. Abenandar comes to the scene and tells one of the soldiers that it's obvious Jesus cannot go on and he commands the soldiers to "Help him." Simon of Cyrene walks by with his little son. Simon sees the pitiful, bleeding Jesus lying on the ground. The little boy also sees the awful sight and cries "Abba." Simon begins to usher the boy away when suddenly the soldiers notice him. They indeed "press" him into service. Simon proceeds to walk away saying this is not any of his business. Even a woman from the crowd urges him to help Jesus saying, "He is a holy man." The soldiers insist that Simon carry Jesus' cross. The character unwillingly agrees. Now that he is forced to carry a cross like a criminal, Simon feels it is necessary to let everyone know that he is not a criminal, "Remember, I am an innocent man, forced to carry the cross of a condemned man." Simon's statement is very ironic given the context of the film. He contrasts his innocence with Jesus' "guilt"—when, in fact, the spiritual reality is completely the other way around.

Simon picks up the cross only with great resentment. When the weight of it is placed upon him and Jesus joins him beneath it, Simon looks at Jesus rather scornfully as if to say, "What am I doing here with you?" As they progress on the way together Jesus falls. Simon tries to hold Him up, but cannot. The soldiers begin to mercilessly kick and beat Jesus. Simon, still holding the cross, looks on. We see the character struggle in his conscience. Suddenly he throws off the cross and yells at the soldiers to stop their brutality. Moved with pity for the beaten criminal, Simon intercedes on His behalf. He threatens the guards that unless they stop hitting Christ he will no longer carry the cross and even says that he doesn't care what they do to him. Amazingly the character is willing to suffer in defense of Christ. The soldiers burst out in laughter. A few of them are drinking. With mockery they agree to Simon's request. The cross is picked up and placed back on Simon's shoulder. As Simon begins to lift it once again, a soldier comes up to him and calls him "Jew!" This is the only time in the movie that any character is so identified—and it is not the Jewish leaders—but a man who helps Jesus on the way to Calvary.

The Spiritual Lesson

As Jesus and Simon walk away the camera focuses on their arms intertwined over the cross. It is very obvious that Simon and Jesus carry the cross together and also very obvious that many times it is Simon who literally carries the weight of the whole cross. Very oddly, Jesus is actually, literally aided in His task. This is a very important theological point.

Simon of Cyrene is given a cross he did not want, did not look for and was absolutely loath to embrace. And that's just the way the spiritual life is. God sends crosses not of our choosing and we hate it and complain about it. There are some kinds of suffering that are completely unexpected, like the sudden death of a loved one, a diagnosis of cancer or loss of employment. We can either endure these sufferings with resentment or enter into them with Christ.

Through the literal carrying of the cross, Jesus and Simon

have become one. Simon has been allowed to enter into the Passion with Him. When Jesus falters on the way and crumples to the ground, Simon tries to hold Him up. Simon encourages Jesus with the words, "We're nearly there. Almost there. Almost done." The words have a double meaning. On the surface Simon intends to just say to Jesus, "We are almost at Calvary—and you won't have to be carrying this awful cross much longer." But ultimately Simon tells Jesus that His salvific task is nearly fulfilled. His words, "Almost done," echo Christ's words on the cross, "It is accomplished." And it is Simon who supports Jesus in this accomplishment.

When Simon and Jesus finally get to the hill, Jesus crashes face down towards the camera. Simon, bearing the full weight of the cross, growls hideously in a last burst of strength and throws the cross off. He appears to make this effort so that the cross will not crash down on the prostrate Christ. Simon, his own strength spent, falls to his knees. Simon and Jesus look at each other. Simon appears to study Christ—his gaze is long and intent and full of emotion. He has to be coaxed away by the soldiers. But Simon, who initially did not want to be associated with the "criminal," now hesitates to leave Jesus. The soldiers have to drive him off with violence. Simon departs the scene weeping.

The character has undergone a tremendous awakening. At first Jesus was just some criminal that Simon was forced to be associated with and was afraid for his reputation. His life was joined to Christ's in the Lord's redemptive journey. The man that Simon did not want to be with, whose cross was "none of his business," he cannot now leave behind. In the carrying of the cross, Simon was transformed into Christ's helper, defender and advocate.

Carrying the cross is difficult, laborious, exhausting, humiliating and painful. But the Simon of Cyrene episode in *The Passion* illustrates that when one carries his cross in union with

Christ, personal suffering becomes redemptive. Through suffering the person can discover Jesus. Indeed, in the spiritual journey, suffering accepted for the sake of the Lord helps Christ save the world. Saint Paul teaches, "Even now I find my joy in the suffering I endure for you. In my own flesh I make up for what is lacking in the sufferings of Christ for the sake of his body, the Church" (Colossians 1:24).

Traditional Faith

A full year before the Gibson film premiered, a group of scholars, both Christians and Jews, in possession of a stolen script, launched their criticisms of the movie.[21] Known informally as the "scholars group," they accused *The Passion* of anti-Semitism, of not paying attention to modern biblical scholarship and of not adhering to the United States Conference of Catholic Bishops' 1988 guidelines for Passion plays. Paula Fredriksen, a professor of Scripture at Boston University, faulted the movie because it was "a big-budget dramatization of key points of traditionalist theology."[22] Other major voices in non-traditionalist theological circles rejected the film because it paid no attention to modern historical-critical scholarship that has for decades denied the historical authenticity of the Gospel accounts of Jesus life.[23] In an article for *The New Yorker* magazine Gibson responded to the scholars' view:

---

[21] For a full discussion of the controversy see: Paula Fredriksen, "Mad Mel, The Gospel According to Gibson," *The New Republic*, July 28, 2003. For a rebuttal of her criticism of the film see Tom Piatak, "Gibson and His Enemies—ADL and Neo-Catholics Intend to Kill the Film," *Chronicles Magazine*, August 29, 2003.

[22] Fredriksen.

[23] "The Passion Wounds Theologians' Egos," press statement of William Donohue, Catholic League for Religious and Civil Rights, February 23, 2004.

Gibson is unconvinced by such scholarly interpretations [of Scripture]. "They always dick around with it, you know?" he says. "Judas is always some kind of friend of some freedom fighter named Barabbas, you know what I mean? It's horseshit. It's revisionist bullshit. And that's what these academics are into. They gave me notes on a stolen script. I couldn't believe it. It was like they were more or less saying I have no right to interpret the Gospels myself, because I don't have a bunch of letters behind my name. But they are for children, these Gospels. They're for children, they're for old people, they're for everybody in between. They're not necessarily for academics. Just get an academic on board if you want to pervert something."[24]

The irony of Gibson's statement is that the theological content of *The Passion* is not simply his private interpretation. Surely the film is Gibson's faith statement, but precisely for that reason it remains faithful to the Christian teaching. The doctrinal revelation of the Christian religion is the ultimate content of the film. For this reason the film has universal appeal. Moreover, because it is a dramatization, as Fredriksen stated, of "traditionalist faith" on the sacrifice of Christ, the film is naturally filled with those who are opposed to Jesus and those who accept Him and support Him in His mission of redemption. The sacrifice of Christ is the source of the Church—whose members, in The Passion, are gathered together under the cross. Even an unidentified member of the Sanhedrin helps two converted Roman soldiers take Jesus down from the cross. By the radical and complete pouring out of Christ's blood, the old wall of division has been overcome.

---

[24] Peter J. Boyer, "The Jesus War, Mel Gibson and 'The Passion,'" *The New Yorker*, September 15, 2003.

Chapter Five

SOURCES OF *THE PASSION*

T HE *PASSION OF THE CHRIST* is the most theologically informed movie about Jesus ever made. Unlike other
screen adaptations of the Gospels, *The Passion* is filled
with images, gestures and actions—from the opening scene in
the garden of Gethsemane to the resurrection of Jesus at the
film's end—that serve as theological commentary on the redemptive mission of Christ. Much of this theological material may be
called "extra-biblical"—in other words, not literally found in the
New Testament. Some purists may find this kind of theological
license spiritually offensive. However, it is precisely the "extra"
material that makes *The Passion* the religiously important and
engaging movie that it is. The question is not, does Gibson stick
to the Bible? The question is, from the Christian point of view,
does *The Passion* support and express Christian faith? Does the
"extra" material draw the viewer into a deeper awareness of the
meaning of the Christian religion generally and the sacrifice of
Christ specifically? Even from a non-Christian perspective, does
the non-biblical material serve the cinematic focus of the movie
rather than distract from it? This book explains why both questions must be answered in the affirmative.

The Gospels

The Passion is woven together by biblical, liturgical, devotional, doctrinal and theological material. The primary structural element of the film is biblical. The drama of *The Passion* is taken directly from the New Testament. All the scenes recorded in the New Testament are there—including the washing of the disciples' feet, parts of John's farewell discourse and the institution of the Eucharist. Many who have seen the film defend it against the accusation of anti-Semitism by citing the fact that Gibson simply remains faithful to the Gospels. Many are attracted to the film because of its fidelity to Scripture. Not only do biblical scenes form the backbone of the movie, but also much of the action and dialog of these scenes is directly biblical. The major scenes taken from the New Testament are as follows:

Garden of Gethsemane (Matthew 26:36-46, Mark 14:32-42, Luke 22:39-45).

Peter, James, John in the garden (Matthew 26:37, Mark 14:37).

Jesus sweats blood (Luke 22:44).

"Could you not watch one hour with me?" (Matthew 26:40, Mark 14:37).

Jesus betrayed with kiss of Judas (Matthew 26:48, Mark 14:44-45).

"Judas do you betray the Son of Man with a kiss?" (Luke 22:48).

Cutting off the ear of the high priest's servant (Matthew 26:51, Mark 14:47, Luke 22:51).

Peter identified as the one who cuts off the ear of the high priest's servant (John 18:10).

Jesus heals the ear of the high priest's servant (Luke 22:51).

"Those who live by the sword shall die by the sword" (Matthew 26:52).

Trial Before Caiaphas and Sanhedrin (Matthew 26:57-58, Mark 14:53-65, Luke 22:66-71, John 18:12-24).

Witnesses (Matthew 26:59-61, Mark 14:55-59).

Temple guard strikes Jesus for not answering the high priest "properly" (John 18:22-23).

"Are you the Messiah, the Son of the Blessed One?" (Mark 14:61).

High priest tears his garments (Matthew 26:65, Mark 14:63).

Peter's denial (Matthew 26:69-75, Mark 14:66-72, Luke 22:54-62, John 18:12-17)).

Peter's denial foretold (flashback) (Matthew 26:35, Mark 14:31, Luke 22:33, John 14:37).

Judas tries to return the blood money (Matthew 27:3-4).

Judas hangs himself (Matthew 27:5).

Trial Before Pilate (Matthew 27:11-25, Mark 15:1-14, Luke 23:1-7 and 13-25, John 18:28-40 and 19:4-16).

Chief priests and Jews accuse Jesus of crimes (Mark 15:3-5, Luke 23:1-2, 5, John 18:29).

Chief priests and Jews ask for Christ to be crucified (Matthew 27:22-23, Mark 15:13-14, Luke 23:21, John 19:6, 15).

Pilate's wife tells him not to condemn Jesus (Matthew 27:19).

Jews ask for Barabbas (Matthew 27:20, Mark 15:6-8, 15, Luke 23:19, 25, John 18:39-40).

Jesus is sent to Herod (Luke 23:6-12).

Pilate is conflicted (Matthew 27:23-24, Mark 15:14, Luke 23:13-16, 22, John 19:6, 8, 12).

"Let his blood be on us and on our children" (Matthew 27:25).

Pilate washes his hands (Matthew 27:24).

Scourging of Jesus (Matthew 27:26, Mark 15:15, John 19:1).

Jesus is crowned with thorns (Matthew 27:29, Mark 15:17, John 19:2).

Jesus mocked; head beaten with rod, and spat upon (Matthew 27:29-30, Mark 15:18-19, John 19:3).

"Ecce Homo" (John 19:5).

Jesus Carries His Cross (John 19:17).

Simon of Cyrene forced to carry Jesus' cross (Matthew 27:32, Luke 23:26).

Crucifixion and Death of Jesus (Matthew 27:34-56, Mark 15:24-41, Luke 23:33-49, John 19:17-37).

Jesus taunted by Jews and Jewish leaders while on the cross, e.g., "You said you would destroy the Temple and in three days rebuild it; save yourself." (Matthew 27:40, Mark 15:29).

One thief abuses Jesus, the other confesses faith in Jesus (Luke 24:39-43).

"Father forgive them for they know not what they do" (Luke 24:34).

"Eloi, Eloi lama sabacthani" (Matthew 27:46, Mark 15:34).

"Woman behold your son…" (John 19:26-27).

"I thirst" (John 19:28).

Jesus is given to drink from sponge on hyssop (John 19:29).

"It is consummated" (John 19:30).

Legs of the two thieves are broken (John 19:31-33).

Jesus' side is pierced with a lance—blood and water flow out (John 19:34-37).

Roman soldier converted (Matthew 27:54, Mark 15:39, Luke 24.47).

Earthquake (Matthew 27:51).

Veil of the Temple rent in two (Matthew 27:51, Mark 15:38, Luke 23:45).

Jesus Taken Down From the Cross (Matthew 27:59-60, Mark 15:46, Luke 24:53, John 19:38-40).

While all the major scenes in the film are found in Scripture it is obvious that most of them are embellished with theological images, dialog, gestures and actions not found in the Bible. The vast majority of these embellishments are taken directly from, or at least inspired by, the visions of Blessed Anne Catherine Emmerich. The fact is: the Gibson film is dominated by the spiritual experiences of this 19th century Roman Catholic stigmatist and mystic as they are recorded in *The Dolorous Passion of Our Lord Jesus Christ*. The contributions Emmerich makes to Gibson's 21st century movie cannot be overemphasized.

Gibson and Emmerich

Gibson personally credited Emmerich with helping him envision his film. The *Dolorous Passion* is a narrative of her visions recorded by the famous German poet M. Clemens Brentano. Gibson had acquired the library of a convent that closed down. "He says that when he was researching *The Passion* he reached up for a book and Brentano's volume tumbled out of the shelf into his hands. He sat down to read it, and was flabbergasted by the vivid imagery of Emmerich's visions. 'Amazing images,' he said. 'She supplied me with stuff I never would have thought of.' The one image that is most noticeable in *The Passion* is the scene after Jesus' scourging, when a grief-stricken Mary gets down on her knees to mop up his blood."[1]

Anne Catherine Emmerich was a German stigmatist and visionary born on September 8, 1774 in the village of Flamske

---

[1] Peter J. Boyer, "The Jesus War: Mel Gibson and 'The Passion,'" *The New Yorker*, September 15, 2003.

in the German province of Westphalia. Even as a child she was extraordinarily pious and received many visions and spiritual favors. She could, for example, distinguish between objects that were used for either good or evil purposes, she knew when relics or consecrated objects were nearby and was also aware of the presence of the Blessed Sacrament. She felt the attraction of the Blessed Sacrament when a priest carrying a consecrated Host passed by even though he was a great distance from her house. As a youth she already practiced severe asceticism and greatly desired to become a nun. She had a most profound prayer life, a deep, intimate love for Jesus whom she considered her Spouse. When she was twenty-four years old she received the stigmata of the crown of thorns. When she was twenty-eight years old her desire to enter the religious life was at last granted and she entered the Convent of Agnetenberg in Dulmen. She took her final vows on November 13, 1803 at the age of twenty-nine.

Her life in the convent was difficult and unpleasant due to the attitude of the other nuns towards her. Some were envious of her spiritual gifts. Others resented her because she was often ill and burdensome to the convent. However, her many illnesses were often the result of Emmerich spiritually taking on the illnesses of the other nuns. In this sense Anne Catherine was a true victim soul. She also endured the temptations of others so they might be relieved of them.

In December 1811, by order of Jerome Bonaparte, King of Westphalia, her nunnery was suppressed and Anne Catherine was forced to live in the secular world. In December of 1812 she received the full, visible stigmata of Jesus' wounds. She became the subject of formal examinations both by those in the medical profession and the authorities of the Church. Her case was even written up in the Medical Journal of Salzburg in 1814. As a bearer of the stigmata and as a victim soul for others, Anne Catherine's life was filled with extreme physical and spiritual suffering. Her life was characterized by a deep charity for the poor and afflicted. Moreover, all kinds of people, of high and low rank, sought her spiritual advice and her prayers. She was often in a state of ecstasy and the wounds of her stigmata often bled profusely, especially on Fridays. After extreme physical sufferings, that lasted about three weeks, Anne Catherine died on February 9, 1824.

A person who had taken great interest in her during her life wrote as follows:

> After her death, I drew near her bed. She was sup-
> ported by pillows, lying on her left side.... The ex-
> pression on her countenance was perfectly sublime,
> and bore the traces of the spirit of self-sacrifice, the
> patience and resignation of her whole life; she looked
> as though she had died for the love of Jesus, in the
> very act of performing some work of charity for oth-
> ers. For the last time I took in mine the hand marked
> with a sign so worthy of our utmost veneration, the
> hand which was as a spiritual instrument in the in-
> stant recognition of whatever was holy... the chari-
> table, industrious hand, which had so often fed the
> hungry and clothed the naked—this hand was now
> cold and lifeless. A great favor had been withdrawn
> from the earth. God had taken from us the hand of
> his spouse, who had rendered testimony to, prayed,
> and suffered for the truth. It appeared as though it
> had not been without meaning, that she had resign-
> edly laid down upon her bed the hand which was the
> outward expression of a particular privilege granted
> by Divine grace.[2]

Six weeks after her burial it was believed that her body had

---

[2] From the "Life of Anne Catherine Emmerich," in Anne Catherine Emmerich, *The Dolorous Passion of Our Lord Jesus Christ*, TAN Books, Rockford, IL, 1983, pp. 54-55.

been stolen. This necessitated that her grave be opened and her body exhumed. With seven witnesses present, Anne Catherine's body was discovered. It was completely incorrupt. She was beatified by Pope John Paul II on October 3, 2004.

The Images From Emmerich

The Passion of the Christ is saturated with images from Emmerich's visions. One critic of the movie stated, "*The Passion of the Christ* is a film version of Emmerich's imaginative interpretation of the Gospels. The film is so dependent upon her that it could have been aptly titled *The Passion According to Emmerich*."[3] This is a very accurate observation. The film's structure is biblically based. However, Emmerich's visions are also biblically based. It is entirely possible that the Gibson film is a direct adaptation of Emmerich's *Dolorous Passion*. In no sense do I mean this as a criticism. The Gospels are meant to be interpreted. Some might prefer Scorsese's revisionist point of view or that of Tim Rice and Andrew Lloyd Weber in *Jesus Christ Superstar* to the point of view of a devout and holy nun. When we say that the Gibson movie is based on Emmerich—this is simply to understand the movie. Furthermore I am not saying that the entire movie was inspired by Emmerich—but a great deal of what the viewer sees on film can be found in the account of Emmerich's visions, perhaps as much as seventy percent.

How indebted Gibson is to Emmerich may be demonstrated by an examination of the opening scene of his movie. The movie begins in the garden of Gethsemane bathed in moonlight. Emmerich describes the scene: "The moon had risen, and already gave light in the sky, although the earth was still dark."[4] The film's

---

[3] Philip A. Cunningham, "Gibson's *The Passion of the Christ:* A Challenge to Catholic Teaching," at www.bs.edu, February 25, 2004.

opening scene, Christ's agony in the garden, is dominated by the conflict between Christ and Satan. This conflict is right out of Emmerich. Satan tempts Jesus in every possible way, including the temptation that appears in the movie that Jesus is not capable of bearing the sins of men.

> He fell on his face, overwhelmed with unspeakable sorrow, and all the sins of the world displayed themselves before him, under countless forms, and in all their real deformity. He took them all upon himself, and in his prayer offered his own adorable Person to the justice of his Heavenly Father, in payment for so awful a debt. But Satan, who was enthroned amid all these horrors, and even filled with diabolical joy at the sight of them, let loose his fury against Jesus, and displayed before the eyes of his soul increasingly awful visions, at the same time addressing his adorable humanity in words such as these: "Takest thou even these sins upon thyself? Art thou willing to bear its penalty? Art thou prepared to satisfy for all these sins?" (…) The remainder of the grotto was filled with frightful visions of our crimes; Jesus took them all upon himself, but that adorable Heart, which was so filled with the perfect love for God and man, was flooded with anguish, and overwhelmed beneath the weight of so many abominable crimes (DP, 100-101).

As in Scripture and Emmerich's visions, Jesus in the movie approaches the slumbering Peter, James and John. When they are awakened in the movie they seemed disturbed at Jesus's appearance and ask themselves what is the matter with Him. This reaction of the three apostles is in Emmerich and she inspires

---

[4] Emmerich, p. 99. For the convenience of the reader all other references to the *Dolorous Passion* will be noted at the end of each paragraph where her work is cited.

the film's dialog: "John said to him: 'Master what has befallen thee? Must I call the other disciples? Ought we to take flight?' Jesus answered him: "Call not the eight; I did not bring them hither, because they could not see me thus agonizing without being scandalized; they would yield to temptation, forget much of the past, and lose their confidence in me" (DP, 104).

In *The Passion* this dialog is stripped down. The disciples ask if the others should be summoned, and Jesus replies, "I don't want them to see me like this."

In Emmerich Jesus suffers great anguish about His mission because He sees all of the heresies, corruption, scandals, faults, injustices and sins of the future Church and the great ingratitude of men. It was rumored that in the original version of *The Passion* Jesus saw some of these injustices displayed before His eyes.

The way Christ looks in the agony in the garden scene fits Emmerich's description: "[B]y the light of the moon, they saw him standing before them, his face pale and bloody, and his hair in disorder, their weary eyes did not at the first moment recognize him for he was indescribably changed" (DP, 118). (At this point I should add that Jesus' face, especially as it appears in the garden, looks very much like the Christ of the Shroud of Turin. It would seem that Gibson aimed for this look.) Also consistent with Emmerich, the Christ of *The Passion* sweats blood and falls down on His face in the garden. Also very theologically important, Emmerich describes Jesus as the New Adam. When God created the first Adam, from his side Eve was formed and she became the "mother of all the living." The one flesh unity of the first man and woman is the sacramental sign of the marriage between Christ and the Church as "Jesus Christ, the second Adam, was pleased also to let sleep come upon him—the sleep of death on the cross, and he was also pleased to let his side be opened, in order that the second Eve, the virgin Spouse, the Church, the mother of all the living might be formed from it" (DP, 109). The

New Adam/New Eve theology is extremely significant as it forms, as we saw in Chapter One, one of the primary themes of Gibson's film.

The arrest of Jesus follows Emmerich very closely. The following details of her visions appear in the Gibson film (and of course overlap with Scripture):

1. Jesus walked up to the soldiers and said in a firm and clear voice, "Whom seek ye?" The leaders answered, "Jesus of Nazareth," Jesus said to them, "I am he."

2. Jesus again asked, "Whom seek ye?" They replied "Jesus of Nazareth." Jesus made answer, "I have told you I am he; if therefore you seek me, let these go their way."

3. Judas therefore approached Jesus and gave him a kiss, saying, "Hail Rabbi."

4. Jesus replied, "What, Judas, do you betray the Son of Man with a kiss?"

5. Judas wishes to flee, but the Apostles would not allow it; they rushed at the soldiers and cried out, "Master shall we strike with the sword?" Peter, who was more impetuous than the rest, seized the sword, and struck Malchus, the servant of the high priest, who wished to drive away the Apostles, and cut off his right ear; Malchus fell to the ground and a great tumult ensued.

6. When Peter struck Malchus, Jesus said to him, "Put up again thy sword into its place; for all that take the sword shall perish with the sword."

7. ...and approaching Malchus, he touched his ear, prayed, and it was healed.

8. Malchus was instantly converted by the cure wrought upon him.

9. The Pharisees, seeing [John] ordered the guards to arrest him... but he ran away... he had slipped off his coat,

that he might escape more easily from the hands of his enemies.

10. They... struck Jesus with knotted cords.

11. The bridge over which they led Jesus was long... when they were half over the bridge they gave full vent to their brutal inclinations, and struck Jesus with such violence that they threw him off the bridge into the water.

It is the last mentioned detail—Jesus being thrown off the bridge—that strikes the viewer as definitely extra-biblical, especially any viewer well acquainted with the New Testament. The viewer may also be shocked to see how horribly the Temple guards treat Jesus. While such ill-treatment is hinted at in the Gospels (Matthew 27:67-68, Mark 14:65, Luke 22:63-65, John 19:22), it is quite explicit in Emmerich's visions. Gibson adds something to Emmerich's vision of Jesus falling over the bridge. In the film Judas is seated below the bridge and is suddenly confronted by the bloody and bruised face of Jesus. Jesus' sudden and ghastly intrusion demonstrates an important point. Judas has fled the garden and is hiding now. He is alone—alone with his sin. That the One whom he betrayed unexpectedly appears and casts His glance upon him shows that Judas cannot escape his sin or his guilt. Though he may try, it will find him. The last time Judas saw Christ's face was in the garden just after he gave Jesus the kiss of betrayal. Jesus' face was beautiful then, but full of sorrow and pity for Judas. Now Judas beholds Jesus' beaten face—but the face is not there to condemn him but to provoke him to repentance and love. However, Judas is already on the side of the Devil. A demon is with him, hidden at first, but his hideous face appears and Judas flees in terror.

This is a good example of how Gibson will take material from Emmerich and rework it for his purposes.

The Trial Before the Sanhedrin

The trial before the Sanhedrin is also studded with material from Emmerich. In Emmerich the trial is divided between a hearing before Annas and then a hearing before Caiaphas. There are also separate hearings in John's Gospel. In *The Passion* these scenes are combined. In the movie a Temple guard pounds on the door of a Jew, rousing him in the middle of the night, and orders him to gather members of the Sanhedrin. The poor and harried man is given a moneybag. The scene insinuates that the money is to be used for bribes. In the Emmerich vision, "They hastened to all the inns to seek out those persons whom they knew to be enemies of our Lord, and offered them bribes in order to secure their appearance" (DP, 143).

During the trial one of the guards strikes Jesus because of the answer Jesus made to a question put to Him by Annas. Emmerich describes the scene thus: "'I have spoken openly to the world, I have always taught in the synagogue, and in the Temple, whither all the Jews resort; and in secret I have spoken nothing. Why askest thou me? Ask them who have heard what I have spoken unto them; behold they know what things I said.' (…) A base menial who was standing near… struck our Lord on the face with an iron gauntlet, exclaiming at the same moment, 'Answerest thou the high priest so?'" This is derived from the Gospel of John. "'Why do you question me? Question those who heard me when I spoke. It should be obvious that they will know what I said.' At this reply, one of the guards who was standing nearby, gave Jesus a sharp blow on the face. 'Is that the way to answer the high priest?' he said" (John 18:21-22). In John, in Emmerich and in the movie Jesus responds, "If I have spoken evil, give testimony of the evil; but if the truth, why do you strike me?"

In Scripture only one accusation by a witness is noted specifically—namely that Jesus said: "Destroy the Temple and in three days I will raise it up" (John 2:19). In addition to this one, Emmerich adds quite a few more accusations including that Jesus cured the sick with the help of the Devil and stated that people must eat His flesh and drink His blood if they are to have eternal life. One by one the witnesses in the Gibson film present these accusations consistent with Emmerich's visions.

In Emmerich only two members of the Sanhedrin protest the proceedings, Joseph of Arimathea and Nicodemus. They are shown in the Gibson film making similar protests—i.e., in Emmerich Nicodemus remarks that the Council was taking place in an "extraordinary and hurried manner" with "malice and envy" as the motives (DP, 161).

The Gibson film follows Emmerich when Caiaphas asks Jesus point blank if He is the Messiah, "the Son of the Living God." Jesus answers, "I am," as recorded in the Gospel of Mark and then, as in Emmerich and the Gospel, Jesus states: "Hereafter you shall see the Son of Man sitting on the right hand of the power of God and coming on the clouds of heaven" (DP, 163). Also, as in Emmerich and the Gospels, Jesus' testimony as to His divine identity causes Caiaphas to rend his garments and call for the death of Jesus.

Soon after Caiaphas pronounces the sentence upon Jesus, He is surrounded by Temple guards and other members of the mob that had gathered and He is immediately subjected to a furious, relentless beating. This scene is echoed in Emmerich: "No sooner did Caiaphas, with the other members of the Council, leave the tribunal than a crowd of miscreants... surrounded Jesus like a swarm of infuriated wasps, and began to heap every imaginable insult upon him" (DP, 164). The group that surrounds Jesus in the film looks just like a "swarm of infuriated wasps."

Some aspects of Gibson's portrayal of the denial of Peter are taken from Emmerich. In the movie Peter witnesses Jesus being beaten. As recorded in Emmerich, Jesus looks at Peter—

"a look of mingled compassion and grief." This look is also recorded in the Gospel of Luke (22:61) by which "Peter remembered the word that the Lord had spoken to him, 'Before the cock crows today you will deny me three times.'" In Emmerich Jesus' glance recalled to Peter's "mind in the most forcible and terrible manner the words addressed to him by our Lord on the previous evening." In *The Passion* this memory is executed through a flashback immediately after Peter denies Jesus for the third time.

In the Gibson film Peter, consumed with grief, rushes out of the high priest's courtyard and immediately runs into Mary. In distress he falls to his knees, cries out, "Mother," and with tears declares his sin. This scene is taken directly from Emmerich. Also, as in Emmerich: Peter, after his confession, "ran out of the court as if beside himself…" (DP, 174).

Mary in Emmerich and Gibson

The role that Mary plays in the Gibson film is, to a large degree, inspired by Emmerich. Mary, for Emmerich, is deeply, even mystically, connected to her Son. Emmerich's Mary, as in the movie, often accompanies Jesus, with John and Mary Magdalen, and suffers with her Son. Emmerich speaks of Mary "as ever united to her Divine Son by interior spiritual communications; she was, therefore, fully aware of all that happened to him—she suffered with him…. The Blessed Virgin, who ever beheld in spirit the opprobrious treatment her dear Son was receiving, continued to lay up 'all these things in her heart…'" (DP, 172-3). The idea that Mary was fully aware of all that happened to Jesus is shown in the Gibson film from the first instant that we see her. Jesus has been arrested. As the Temple guards bring him bound out of the garden one guard strikes him. This is the very first of many horrible blows that will be inflicted on Christ throughout the movie. The scene cuts directly to Mary who rises with a start as if the blow to her Son awakened her.

In Emmerich, as in the Gibson film, Jesus is confined in a subterranean prison. Emmerich had already stated that "Mary's heart was with her Divine Son" and she hoped that the door to Caiaphas' house would be opened "that she might again have a chance of beholding him, for she knew that [the door] alone separated her from the prison where [Jesus] was confined" (DP, 173). Emmerich continues to say of Mary that "she was with Jesus in spirit, and Jesus was with her…" (DP, 175). This spiritual connection between Mary and Jesus is beautifully dramatized in the movie when Mary seems to miraculously locate just where in the underground prison Jesus is chained. She kneels on the stone pavement, presses her face against it and, as if peering through a crack in the floor, binds her soul to Jesus. The camera takes the viewer below the stone floor and we see Jesus looking upward, aware of His mother's comforting presence.

Just prior to the Last Supper in the *Dolorous Passion*: "Our Lord announced to his Blessed Mother what was going to take place. She besought him, in the most touching terms, to let her die with him" (DP, 72). And when Jesus is on the cross "the Blessed Virgin, filled with intense feelings of motherly love, entreated her Son to permit her to die with him.…" These words from Emmerich's *Dolorous Passion* are the very words of Mary in the film. She says these words when she approaches Jesus on the cross and kisses His bleeding feet. And in the movie, as in Emmerich, these words of Mary are immediately followed by those of Christ who looks at His mother with John standing next to her: "'Woman, behold thy son,' then he said to John, 'Behold thy mother.'"

Finally, the movie, as in Emmerich, has the dead body of Jesus placed in Mary's lap at the foot of the cross:

> The adorable head of Jesus rested upon Mary's knee…
> the Blessed Virgin was overwhelmed with sorrow and

love. Once more, and for the last time, did she hold in her arms the body of her most beloved Son... and she gazed upon his wounds and fondly embraced his blood-stained cheeks, whilst Magdalen pressed her face upon his feet (DP, 316).

The Scourging at the Pillar in Emmerich and Gibson

The scourging of Jesus at the pillar is the most intensely violent episode in the Gibson film. Again, many details in this prolonged scene are lifted out of Emmerich's vision of this horrific torture. Faithful to the 19th century stigmatist, Pilate in the movie, prompted by his wife's concerns for Christ, decides to have Jesus scourged, hoping that a severe punishment will appease the Jewish leaders. The Roman soldiers who scourge Jesus and soldiers who attend the beating are depicted in the Gibson film as merciless, ignorant brutes. Emmerich describes them as resembling "wild beasts or demons, and appeared to be half drunk" (DP, 218). Indeed, in *The Passion*, when we see the gang of soldiers gather for the scourging, they laugh and carouse with one another and a few of them are drinking from small goblets. They do appear to be at least half drunk. In Emmerich these Roman soldiers are absolutely brutal and they are no less so in the Gibson film. In the Gibson film they certainly relish the opportunity to inflict a beating. In the film the scourging begins with canes. In Emmerich canes are also used first: "[T]hen did two furious ruffians... begin in the most barbarous manner to scourge the sacred body from head to foot. The whips or scourges which they first made use of appeared to me to be made of flexible white wood, but perhaps they were composed of sinews of the ox, or of strips of leather. Our loving Lord, the Son of God, true God and true Man, writhed as a worm under the blows of these barbarians; his mild but deep groans might be heard from afar…" (DP, 219).

The canes in the movie are exactly as Emmerich describes them. One of the soldiers even bends the rod to test its flexibility as he says in Latin, "Let's make music." Jesus does writhe under the blows and emits deep groans. In Emmerich Roman guards are stationed all around, just so in the film. After the caning the soldiers switch to a different torture instrument. At first they pick up a club studded with nails, but the Roman overseer tells them no—use the whips instead. The audience is relieved. This "species of thorny stick," while we only see them in the movie, are actually used in Emmerich's vision. But like the movie, the soldiers also use "straps covered with iron hooks, which penetrated to the bone, and tore off large pieces of flesh at every blow" (DP, 221). Indeed, this very effect of the instrument is very graphically depicted in the Gibson movie. In Emmerich Jesus' body is turned over so the scourging may continue on the "fresh" side. So too in the Gibson film, and undoubtedly this was the common practice in the Roman method of scourging.[5]

Emmerich says that "the body of our Lord was completely torn to shreds—it was but one wound" (DP, 221). Indeed, by the end of the scourging Jesus' body looks just like "one wound" in *The Passion*.

Emmerich says that the ground "was bathed with his blood." So too in the Gibson film.

During the scourging Jesus looks at His mother. So too in the Gibson film. During the scourging one of the most unexpected and fascinating gestures occurs. Pilate's wife approaches Mary and Mary Magdalen and presents Mary with white linens. After the scourging is over the two Marys drop to their knees in the now abandoned and bloody courtyard, and begin to mop up

---

[5] Gibson studied the Roman method of scourging and crucifixion, notably a famous clinical investigation, "On the Physical Death of Jesus Christ," *Journal of the American Medical Association*, 1986, as quoted by Peter Boyer, "The Jesus War, Mel Gibson and the Passion," *The New Yorker* magazine, September 13, 2003.

the blood of Jesus. Mary uses the linens that Claudia gave to her. This scene is completely inspired by Emmerich.

> When Jesus fell down at the foot of the pillar, after the flagellation, I saw Claudia Procles, the wife of Pilate, send some large pieces of linen to the Mother of God.... I soon after saw Mary and Mary Magdalen approach the pillar where Jesus had been scourged; the mob were at a distance, and they were partly concealed by the other holy women.... They knelt down on the ground near the pillar, and wiped up the sacred blood with the linen which Claudia Procles had sent (DP, 225).

A few minor details have been changed, e.g., in the Gibson film Pilate's wife offers the linens personally and there are no other holy women present at the scourging. In the film, Mary Magdalen uses her veil to wipe up Christ's blood. But, the substance of Emmerich's vision has been translated to film.

Of course in *The Passion* there are several additions to Emmerich's view of the scourging. For example, Gibson has Caiaphas and a few other members of the Sanhedrin observe the torture and, of course, let us not overlook the brilliant image of Satan and the demon child.

Major Images

Several of the most important images and episodes in *The Passion of the Christ* are from Emmerich's visions. One of these episodes, embellished by Gibson, is central to the movie's theme. When Jesus falls again on His way to Calvary, Mary rushes to Him to support and comfort Him. Her presence enables Him to rise and continue the journey to the hill where He will be crucified. In the film Mary asks John to find a way for her to be near Jesus. John negotiates a route. On the way Mary hesitates in a doorway. All of this is recorded in the *Dolorous Passion*:

> [M]ary could not resist her longing to behold her be-loved Son once more, and she begged John to take her to some place through which he must pass. John con-ducted her to a palace, which had an entrance to that street that Jesus traversed after his first fall.... John asked and obtained leave from a kind-hearted servant to stand at the entrance mentioned above.... After praying fervently, [M]ary turned to John and said, "Shall I remain? Ought I go away? Shall I have the strength to support such a sight?" John made answer, "If you do not remain to see him pass, you will grieve afterwards." They remained therefore near the door, with their eyes fixed on the procession, which was still distant, but advancing by slow degrees.... Then came her Beloved Son. He was almost sinking under the heavy weight of the cross, and his head, still crowned with thorns, was drooping in agony on his shoulder. He cast a look of compassion and sorrow upon his Mother, staggered, and fell for the second time upon his hands and knees. Mary was perfectly agonized at this sight; she forgot all else; she saw neither soldiers or executioners; she saw nothing but her dearly be-loved Son; and springing from the doorway into the midst of the group who were insulting and abusing him, she threw herself on her knees by his side and embraced him. The only words I heard were, "Beloved Son!" and "Mother!" but I do not know whether these words were really uttered, or whether they were only in my mind (DP, 254-255).

Gibson's adaptation of the stigmatist's vision created one

of the most moving scenes in the entire film. When Mary is hesitating in the doorway, she sees Jesus fall. This prompts her to
recall a time when Jesus was a small boy and He fell and hurt
Himself. Mary rushed to Him then to comfort Him. By this
memory Mary finds the courage to leave the doorway and comfort her Son again and tell Him, as she had when He was a child,
"I'm here!" Jesus responds with the line from the Book of Revelation: "Behold, Mother, I make all things new"—the line that
serves as the central defining theological statement of the film.

Emmerich inspires even the climax of *The Passion of the
Christ*. Many of the Roman soldiers who appear by name in the
Gibson film are found in Emmerich's visions. One of them is
Cassius. He first appears in *The Passion* with another Roman soldier. Both of them are on horseback. Mary Magdalen entreats
them to intervene in Jesus' case, that the Temple guards have
arrested an innocent man. Cassius appears on film from time to
time as one of the soldiers who escorts Jesus on the Via Dolorosa
and he is the soldier who inquires as to the identity of Jesus'
mother after Mary rushes to her Son and embraces Him on the
path. And at the cross Cassius is the character who pierces Jesus'
side with the lance.

In Emmerich Cassius is described as squinty-eyed and nervous, one "who often excited the derision of his companions"
(DP, 304). The character in the movie is rather puny for a soldier. He also appears to be rather "squinty-eyed" and he does
not seem to have the respect of the other soldiers as he is often
addressed by them in a scornful tone. In Emmerich, as in *The
Passion*, Cassius pierces Jesus' side with a lance. The scene in
the *Dolorous Passion* is described this way:

> [Cassius], taking his lance in both hands, thrust it so
> completely into the right side of Jesus that the point
> went through the heart and appeared on the left side.
> When Cassius drew the lance out of the wound a

quantity of blood and water rushed from it, and flowed over his face and body. This species of washing produced effects somewhat similar to the vivifying waters of Baptism; grace and salvation at once entered his soul. He leaped from his horse, threw himself upon his knees, struck his breast, and confessed loudly before all his firm belief in the divinity of Jesus (DP, 304).

In the Gibson movie this character takes a similar shower and falls on his knees. It is an intense, beautiful, and unexpected moment.

Scripture does speak of a Roman centurion who was converted upon the death of Christ (Matthew 28:54, Mark 15:39, Luke 23:47). In Emmerich this person is Abenadar. This character is also featured in the Gibson film. Emmerich describes his conversion with great detail (DP, 292-293). In the Gibson movie his conversion is only hinted at when, after the great flow of blood and water, Abenadar takes off his helmet in tribute to Jesus.

The following list chronicles the items that appear in *The Passion of the Christ* taken from *The Dolorous Passion of Our Lord Jesus Christ*, or at least inspired by this account of her visions. Certainly this rather obscure mystic had no idea that when she dictated her visions to Brentano they would someday be the source of a major motion picture seen by millions of people all over the world. Needless to say, this list demonstrates that *The Passion* can rightfully be called Emmerich's film:

1. Moonlit garden.
2. Devil in the garden, Jesus tempted.
3. Jesus' dialog with Peter, James, and John in the garden.
4. The manner of Jesus' arrest.
5. Manner of John's escape from the Temple guards.

6. Jesus abused by the Temple guards.
7. Jesus thrown off a bridge.
8. Mary aware of Jesus' sufferings.
9. Mary and Mary Magdalen living together.
10. Mary, Mary Magdalen and John always together.
11. Dialog, characters and proceedings of Jesus' trial before the Sanhedrin.
12. Manner of Peter's denial of Jesus.
13. Peter's confession to Mary; he calls her "Mother."
14. Jesus in subterranean prison; Mary mystically finding him there.
15. Dialog between Judas and Caiaphas when Judas tries to give back the money.
16. Judas harassed by demons and Satan.
17. Judas driven out of town to a desolate spot.
18. The donkey carcass behind Judas.
19. Pilate's wife entreating Pilate to not condemn Jesus.
20. Pilate admonishing the Jewish leaders about Jesus' condition.
21. The private conversation between Jesus and Pilate, ending with Pilate saying, "Truth. What is truth?"
22. The corrupt and effeminate nature of Herod.
23. Herod asking Jesus if He is a king.
24. Herod's treatment of Jesus—dismissing Him as a fool.
25. Physical qualities and brutish nature of the Roman soldiers.
26. Manner of the scourging at the pillar.
27. Use of white-colored canes first, followed by whips studded with sharp metal.
28. Merciless nature of the beating.
29. Jesus looking at His Mother.
30. Soldiers inebriated.
31. Jesus beaten on both sides of his body.
32. Jesus' body torn to shreds.

33. Scourging interrupted.
34. The pavement bathed in His blood.
35. The soldiers' taking delight in their cruelty.
36. Claudia Procles giving Mary linens.
37. Mary and Mary Magdalen wiping up Jesus' blood.
38. Jesus' physical appearance in the "Ecce Homo" scene.
39. Jesus embracing His cross.
40. Mary rushing to Jesus to comfort Him on the path to Calvary.
41. The manner of Simon's refusal to carry the cross.
42. Dialog and manner of Seraphia (Veronica) wiping the face of Jesus.
43. Roman soldiers interrupting the aid Veronica gives to Jesus.
44. Simon protesting the Roman soldiers' abuse of Jesus.
45. Simon supporting Jesus, holding Him up so He won't fall.
46. Simon hesitating to leave Jesus—has to be driven off.
47. Details of the nailing of Jesus' hand.
48. Jesus' arm being violently stretched to meet the pre-drilled hole.
49. The manner of the raising of the cross—falls with a crash into the hole.
50. Jesus' blood splattering on the soldiers.
51. Mary's words to Jesus on the cross.
52. Manner in which Jesus' side is pierced.
53. Cassius takes a shower in the water and blood gushing forth from Christ's side.
54. Cassius falls to his knees and is converted.
55. Abenadar is converted.
56. Earthquake shakes the Temple.
57. Annas' and Caiaphas' reaction to the earthquake.
58. The manner of Jesus' descent from the cross.
59. Bloody crown of thorns and the nails set aside.
60. Jesus' body placed in Mary's lap.

Emmerich and the Jews

In *The Passion of the Christ* Caiaphas and other Jewish leaders are relentless in their efforts to have Jesus crucified. Even though most of the Jewish leaders are played by Italian actors, including Caiaphas, these characters act and look very Jewish—or at least they seem to fulfill a mainstream idea of what first-century, Middle-eastern Jews are supposed to look like. It is very obvious that the Jewish leaders are the enemies of Christ. Many critics of the film have accused Anne Catherine Emmerich of anti-Semitism. Since the Gibson film relies so heavily on Emmerich, it too has been suspected of an anti-Semitic point of view.

It is quite true that Emmerich had little sympathy for what she often calls "the enemies of our Lord," namely: Annas, Caiaphas, the Pharisees as a group, and the crowd of Jews who call for Jesus' death. But it is very wrong to accuse Emmerich of imputing universal guilt to the Jews for the death of Jesus. Moreover, there is very little in her visions to suggest that the guilt of Christ's death is visited upon Jews collectively throughout subsequent generations. Indeed, even more than in Gibson's film, Emmerich shows many individual Jews and even whole groups of Jews very sympathetic to Jesus and disgusted with the unjust treatment He receives. After Jesus is arrested He is taken through the town of Ophel where He performed many miracles. "Cries and lamentations arose on all sides; the poor women and children ran back and forth, weeping and wringing their hands; and calling to mind all the benefits they received from our Lord" (DP, 139). Emmerich acknowledges that Jesus had many friends among the Jewish Council, friends that the Pharisees tried to prevent from attending His trial (DP, 142). During the trial many who watch the proceedings are converted by Jesus' peaceful and patient behavior. Even Temple guards give an excuse for leaving the scene, so repulsed were they at the abuse Jesus was made to endure (DP, 161). Some of the witnesses, whom Emmerich describes as belonging "to the upper classes were less hardened than the others; their consciences were racked with remorse, and they… left the room as quickly as possible" (DP, 165). Pharisees favorable to Jesus are expelled from the Sanhedrin (DP, 180). A Jew whom Jesus had cured of his blindness rushes to the pillar and severs the cords which bind Jesus—thus halting the scourging (DP, 222). In the movie it is the Roman centurion, Abenadar, who brings the beating to an end.

During Jesus' walk to Calvary a group of Jews on their way to the Temple express concern and compassion for Him (DP, 256). Women and children weep for Jesus on the Via Dolorosa (DP, 262). The account of Emmerich's visions is peppered throughout with Jews who show sympathy for Christ. They are often contrasted with the Jews who express hatred toward Him or a lack of compassion. Thirty horsemen from Judea on their way to Jerusalem for the festival see Jesus hanging on the cross and are outraged by it. "When they beheld Jesus hanging on the Cross, saw the cruelty with which he had been treated, and remarked the extraordinary signs of God's wrath which overspread the face of nature, they were filled with horror…" (DP, 290). Many Jews assembled at the crucifixion scene are overcome with grief—knowing Jesus to be an innocent man and the Pharisees gathered there had to "assume a more humble tone, for they feared an insurrection among the people, being well aware of the great existing excitement among the inhabitants of Jerusalem" (DP, 290).

Film critic, Roger Ebert defended *The Passion* against the charge of anti-Semitism: "Gibson's film is not anti-Semitic, but reflects a range of behavior on the part of its Jewish characters, on balance favorably."[6]

This "range" is certainly present in Emmerich's visions.

If the chief priests are portrayed very negatively by

---

[6]   Roger Ebert, "The Passion of the Christ," *Chicago Sun-Times*, February 24, 2004.

Emmerich, the Roman soldiers don't come off looking so good either. In fact, most of them have no redeeming qualities whatever. They are gross, ill-mannered, cruel, merciless barbarians who often are described as drunk, poke fun at Jesus, mock Him and take total delight in causing Jesus unbelievable torment. Gibson captured the depraved character of these soldiers wonderfully. Moreover, Pilate certainly is no hero in Emmerich's visions. He is "weak minded," "debauched and undecided," a vacillator, "excessively superstitious and when in any difficulty given over to charms and spells" whose priority was to "entail no risk to himself." In Emmerich and in the Gibson movie Pilate does try to spare Jesus death by crucifixion primarily because his wife asks him to. Also, Gibson, faithful to Emmerich, provides the reason why Pilate, even though he knows Jesus is innocent, finally gives in to the wishes of the Jewish leaders. Pilate is afraid the Emperor will think he encourages insurrections (DP, 235). This idea is at least hinted at in the Gospel of Matthew. Pilate having received the message from his wife and not convinced that Jesus deserves to die, nonetheless realizes "that he was making no impression [upon the Jews] and a riot was breaking out instead" (Matthew 27:34).

There is one difference between Emmerich's depiction of the Jews and the Romans. The Jewish leaders are often spoken of as being induced to reject Jesus by Satan and demons. For example the chief priests are described as

> ...those most bitter enemies of her Divine Son. They were decked in flowing robes; but ah, terrible to say, instead of appearing resplendent in their character of priests of the Most High, they were transformed into priests of Satan, for no one could look upon their wicked countenances without beholding there, portrayed in vivid colors, the evil passions with which their souls were filled—deceit, infernal cunning, and

a raging anxiety to carry out that most tremendous of crimes, the death of our Lord and Savior, the only Son of God (DP, 187).

Let His Blood Be on Us

Much has been made of one particular line in the movie: "Let his blood be on us and on our children." In Matthew, Pilate "washed his hands in front of the crowd, declaring as he did so, 'I am innocent of the blood of this just man. The responsibility is yours.' The whole people said in reply, 'Let his blood be on us and on our children'" (Matthew 27:24-25). In *The Passion* this line is uttered only by Caiaphas, and to mitigate the charge of anti-Semitism, Gibson did not have it subtitled. It is this line, perhaps more than any other found in the New Testament, that some Christians in past ages used to justify persecution of the Jews.

Apparently, even Emmerich—like many of her contemporaries—had some strange ideas about Jews. In 1819 Emmerich had a vision of an old Jewish woman who took her spirit to a distant Jewish city:

> The soul of the old Jewess Meyr told me on the way that it was true that in former times the Jews, both in our country and elsewhere, had strangled many Christians, principally children, and used their blood for all sort of superstitious and diabolical practices. She had once believed it lawful; but she now knew that it was diabolical murder. They still follow such practices in this country and in others more distant; but very secretly, because they are obliged to have commercial intercourse with Christians.[7]

---

[7] Carl E. Schmoger, *The Life and Revelations of Anne Catherine Emmerich*, TAN Books, Rockford, IL, 1976, pp. 547-548.

Even saintly people can have wrong ideas and be influenced by their own times. The charge that Jews committed ritual murder was widely believed for centuries in Europe. This blood libel was the basis of the trial of Mendel Beilis in early 20th century Russia, and is still promoted by some people in Saudi Arabia and elsewhere. Some critics of the film cite this passage to prove the anti-Semitic roots of *The Passion*. However, it is interesting to consider Emmerich's vision of the verse: "Let his blood be upon us and on our children." She saw those in the crowd tormented by fiery swords and darts. She saw the curse penetrate to the very marrow of their bones—even to the unborn infants. "They appear to be encompassed on all sides by darkness; the words they utter take, in my eyes, the form of black flames, which recoil upon them, penetrating the bodies of some, and only playing around others" (DP, 240). Emmerich says that those Jews in the crowd that the flames only played around, converted after the death of Jesus due to the prayers of Jesus and Mary.

First, we should notice that not all the Jews in the crowd appear to be subject to the curse. Secondly, and most importantly, there is very little to suggest in Emmerich's visions that she believed in or defended the collective guilt of the Jews. Only one statement is made that future generations might be affected and that has to do with unborn children already present at the trial of Jesus.

But the blood of Jesus doesn't just affect the Jewish crowd. Even Pilate, a non-Jew, is subject to a curse. Pilate is as guilty of the blood of Jesus as the Jews who asked for His death. In Emmerich, Pilate is afraid that the Jews will make a complaint about Jesus directly to the Emperor:

> This menace terrified him, and he determined to accede to their wishes, although firmly convinced in his own mind of the innocence of Jesus, and perfectly conscious that by pronouncing sentence of death upon

him he should violate every law of justice, beside breaking the promise he had made to his wife in the morning. Thus did he sacrifice Jesus to the enmity of the Jews, and endeavor to stifle remorse by washing his hands before the people, saying, "I am innocent of the blood of this just man; look you to it." Vainly dost thou pronounce these words, O Pilate! For his blood is on thy head likewise; thou canst not wash his blood from thy soul, as thou dost from thy hands (DP, 242).

In Emmerich, God's wrath is not particular. It affects not only the Jews who oppose Christ, but the pagans as well.

St. Bridget and the Venerable Mary of Agreda

A few of the images and gestures found in *The Passion of the Christ* come from other female mystics. It is noteworthy that Emmerich of the early 19th century, Mother Mary of Agreda, a Spanish nun of the 17th century, and St. Bridget of Sweden of the 14th century, have the very same, or extremely similar private revelations of Jesus' Passion. It may be that Mary of Agreda and Emmerich had access to the writings of St. Bridget and were influenced by her or other visionaries who had similar experiences. In addition, many of the extra-biblical incidents and details found in these visions are present in widely-disseminated devotions and traditions—e.g., Veronica's veil. Or perhaps the similarity of the visions can be spiritually accounted for. There is one truth and God lets these special friends of His see it the same way. In any case the similarities are uncanny.

In St. Bridget's private revelations Jesus looks at Mary during the scourging similar to the vision of Emmerich. Moreover, St. Bridget also sees that, after the scourging, Mary and Mary Magdalen "knelt down before the pillar to which he had been attached and, with some cloth, they reverently soaked up every drop of the Precious Blood of the Savior."[8] It is incredible that all three mystics see the pre-drilled nail holes in the cross and describe how Jesus' left hand was stretched to fit over the hole.

For some of the most disturbing images and gestures in the film, Gibson leaves the main highway of Emmerich and makes a side trip to Venerable Mary of Agreda. Several details of this mystic's visions are incorporated into Gibson's depiction of the crucifixion. When Jesus is nailed to the cross the camera shows the nails driven all the way through the wood. Their points pierce through the back of the cross. This is from Mary of Agreda. Also, another image in the film, horrific and unexpected: the Roman soldiers turn the cross over with Jesus nailed to it. The audience expects that Jesus will crash to the ground with the weight of the cross upon Him. However, the cross does not touch the earth. This too is from Mary of Agreda, recorded in her *Mystical City of God*:

> After the Savior was nailed to the Cross the executioners judged it necessary to bend the points of the nails which projected through the back of the wood, in order that they might not be loosened and drawn out by the weight of the body. For this purpose they raised up the Cross in order to turn it over so that the body of the Lord would rest face downward upon the ground with the weight of the Cross upon Him. The new cruelty appalled all the bystanders and a shout of pity arose in the crowd. But the sorrowful and compassionate Mother intervened by her prayers, and asked the Eternal Father not to permit this boundless outrage to happen in the way the executioners had

---

[8] St. Bridget of Sweden, in *The Life of Mary as Seen By the Mystics*, Raphael Brown, Bruce Publishing Company, Milwaukee, 1951, p. 232.

intended. She commanded her holy angels to come to the assistance of their Creator. When, therefore, the executioners raised up the Cross to let it fall, with the crucified Lord face downward upon the ground, the holy angels supported Him and the Cross above the stony and fetid ground, so that His divine countenance did not come in contact with the rocks and pebbles.[9]

The visions of these Christian holy women are the primary reason why *The Passion of the Christ* is very different from any other film treatment of Jesus' life. Gibson's screen adaptation of what they saw makes *The Passion* the fascinating, unique and theologically rich movie that it is. How true that these Catholic holy women gave him "stuff" he never would have thought of.

Why Did Jesus Die?

Some reviews of *The Passion* expressed a concern that the movie presents a false, or at least inadequate, idea of the reason why Jesus suffered. For example, one critique of the film states: "Finally, the film's graphic, persistent, and intimate violence raises theological questions from a Catholic perspective. It closely resonates with an understanding of salvation that holds that God had to be satisfied or appeased for the countless sins of humanity by subjecting his son to unspeakable torments. This sadistic picture of God is hardly compatible with the God proclaimed by Jesus as the one who seeks for the lost sheep, who welcomes back the prodigal son before he can express remorse, or who causes the rain to fall on the just and the unjust alike."[10]

---

[9] Mother Mary of Agreda, *The Mystical City of God*, Chap. 22, Par. 675, trans. by Fiscar Marison, Corcoran Publishing Co., Albuquerque, NM, 1914, p. 652.

[10] Cunningham.

But redemption is not a free ride. After all, this is the same Jesus who often proclaimed that His death was the cause of salvation (Matthew 26:28, Luke 24:26, John 3:14-16, 12:24), that He would give His life "as a ransom for the many" (Mark 10:45), and that His death would be a stumbling block to faith (Matthew 16:22-23). The entire New Testament, including the Acts of the Apostles, the epistles and the Book of Revelation teaches that Christ's death was necessary for salvation.

The greatest theologians throughout the history of Christianity have pondered why salvation was achieved through the sacrifice of God's Son. One of the most famous answers to this question was given by St. Anselm, a 12th century theologian, in his work "*Cur Deus Homo?*" or "Why Did God Become Man?"

Gibson relied so heavily on Emmerich that perhaps we should consider her view of Christ's suffering as presented in the *Dolorous Passion*. She expresses a very popular and time-honored theological perspective known as the satisfaction theory.[11] In this theory, consistent with St. Anselm, God is a God of mercy, but also a God of justice. He cannot just forgive sin, but the balance of injustice must be "satisfied." Jesus takes the sins of the world upon Himself and the punishment for sin—namely death. Jesus' death is a free offering. He freely offers Himself up as a sacrifice for sin. He turns Himself over to the structures of injustice and iniquity and fills these dark places with Himself—thus overcoming death with life.

Emmerich describes the meaning of Christ's suffering:

Angels came and showed him, in a series of visions, all the sufferings he was to endure in order to expiate sin; how great was the beauty of man, the image of

---

[11] For an excellent discussion on the Gibson film and the satisfaction theory, see Fr. Romanus Cessario, OP, "Gibson's 'Passion' Biblically Exact and Theologically Correct (Gibson must have read Question 48 of the third part of Aquinas)", www.zenit.com, April 8, 2004.

God, before the fall, and how that beauty was changed and obliterated when sin entered the world. He beheld how all sins originated in that of Adam, the signification and essence of concupiscence. Its terrible effects on the powers of the soul, and likewise the signification and essence of all the sufferings entailed by concupiscence. They showed him the satisfaction which he would have to offer the Divine Justice, and how it would consist of a degree of suffering in his soul and body which would comprehend all the sufferings due to the concupiscence of all mankind, since the debt of the whole human race had to be paid by that humanity which alone was sinless—the humanity of the Son of God (DP, 106-107).

Emmerich says that Jesus was so overwhelmed by this burden of sin that "sweat issued forth from all the pores of his body" (DP, 107).

The critics of the Gibson film do not seem to like the idea that justice needed to be repaid, or at least restored. The satisfaction theory of redemption is but a theory, and theologians have reflected on other possible explanations for the Incarnation of Jesus and His Passion. However, the satisfaction theory is not without its logic and strengths. It does not see God as a vengeful judge. This is a caricature of the theory. Rather it ultimately teaches that sin, beginning with Adam and Eve, is a disruption, a tear in the original good creation, which caused man to be alienated from God. The result of this alienation is death. A true reparation is necessary for the new creation to be established, as Jesus states: "Behold, I make all things new." Sin as a disruption, sin as a tear, sin as a violence done to the relation between God and man means that when God enters the world of sin, His death will not be peaceful, as death is not really peaceful, but the result of the crimes of man against the kingdom of God.

In the Gibson film Jesus' countenance is altered by sin—"how great was the beauty of man"—now disfigured by the violence of the sins of man. Christ becomes the icon of sinful man—his beauty destroyed. The theme of the movie is given immediately, before any action begins. It opens with Isaiah 53:4: "It was our infirmities that he bore, our sufferings that he endured...."

But the satisfaction theory is not only about justice, and certainly neither is *The Passion of the Christ*. While Jesus might be bearing the sins of the world, He bears them for love of the human race. This is the point of the Gibson film and it is the essence of the Christian religion.

Chapter Six

REACTIONS TO *THE PASSION*

L OVE. HATE. LAUGHTER. TEARS. Anger. Peace. Repulsion.
Attraction. Disturbance and Serenity. *The Passion of the
Christ*—a movie of extremes—produces extreme reactions.
Hardly anyone who views the film leaves it without a deep reaction of *some kind*. It is not a movie that simply entertains and
then conveniently can be left behind and forgotten. I think it can
truthfully be stated that *The Passion*—like suddenly viewing a
tragic car accident on a highway—takes control of the viewer;
the viewer is not in control of it. Since this book is concerned
about the theological meaning of the film, this chapter will primarily focus on how viewers of *The Passion* are affected by its
religious message.

It has been noted in previous chapters that many theologians, religious leaders, film critics and columnists are critical of
Gibson's film. Even before he saw the film, *New York Times*
columnist Frank Rich voiced unmitigated hostility towards it. In
an article printed seven months before the movie's general release, Rich attacked Gibson and *The Passion* for what Rich per-
ceived to be its anti-Semitism, the manner in which Gibson promoted the movie, and he accused Gibson's father of being a ho-
locaust denier. Rich accused Gibson of "Jew-baiting" and of only
inviting those who would be predisposed to like the film to its

pre-screenings.[1] His attacks provoked Gibson to say, "I want his intestines on a stick."[2] A Frank Rich supporter stated:

> Mel Gibson, like any other artist, must eventually face the public and the critics. There is nothing sacrosanct about any movie, book, painting, etc., all of which are fodder for debate and criticism, unless of course you are a Stalinist and don't appreciate that, in an open society, debate is healthy.... Martin Scorsese did not escape scrutiny when he made a movie about Jesus, and he didn't whine about it either. He defended his point of view, and let his work stand on its own. Once this film hits the marketplace, and non-hand-picked audiences have a look at it, we'll all know what it is and it isn't....[3]

And those non-hand-picked audiences made the Gibson film a box-office success way beyond anyone's expectations. The film cost 30 million dollars to make and grossed 370 million dollars (151 million dollars in the United States alone) in far less than a year. It had the most successful debut of any movie released on a Wednesday. Its total box office gross at this writing is only seven million dollars less than the Oscar-winning *The Lord of the Rings: The Return of the King*. Gibson's film is the most successful "R" rated movie ever made and the most successful foreign language film. By all estimates, *The Passion* was a huge financial success.

However the real fruit of *The Passion* and its most inter-

---

[1] Frank Rich, "The Gospel According to Gibson," *The New York Times*, August 1, 2003.

[2] Peter J. Boyer, "The Jesus War: Mel Gibson and 'The Passion'," *The New Yorker*, September 13, 2003.

[3] Reply to Frank Rich posted on the www.freerepublic.com website, August 2, 2003.

esting and intriguing accomplishment is the film's power to radically change people's lives.

The Conversions

Gibson stated in an interview:

> I'm not a preacher, and I'm not a pastor. But I really feel my career was leading me to make this movie. The Holy Ghost was working through me on this film, and I was just directing traffic. I hope this film has the power to evangelize.... Everyone who worked on this movie was changed. There were agnostics and Muslims on the set converting to Christianity.[4]

The Passion of the Christ has produced countless conversions, of many different kinds and on many different levels. But, of course, the movie has had it share of detractors. Many of these negative voices come from the more secularly-minded commentators such as Rich who, when he finally did see the film, described it as a "porn movie," with "orgasmic spurtings of blood and other body fluids."[5] Some critics of *The Passion* grind their axes against Christianity in general and the Catholic Church in particular. One of the most common complaints from such non-Christian commentators is that the movie is grotesquely violent. Some are disgusted by the graphic images, others, like the author Garry Wills, thought the violence was silly. He stated that he and his wife "had to stop glancing furtively at each other for

---

4 David Limbaugh, "Mel Gibson's Passion for 'The Passion,'" *Creators Syndicate, Inc.*, July 8, 2003.
5 Frank Rich, "Mel Gibson Forgives Us for His Sins," *The New York Times*, March 7, 2004.

fear we would burst out laughing."[6] However, many viewers of the film have rightly observed that only through the eyes of faith does the violence of the film make any sense:

> When we come to realize that the violence depicted in the film is punishment Jesus endured for our sake and in our stead, then the film becomes a thing of beauty. Until that time we can never see but some sadomasochist tendency in the violence played out on Jesus Christ. When we do see the truth, the price Jesus paid becomes a thing of beauty that will moisten the driest eye.[7]

New York Times columnist Maureen Dowd hated the movie, calling her critique of it "The Stations of the Crass." She said that Jesus in the movie taught that we are to love those who hate us, but "This is a Mel Gibson film, so you come out wanting to kick someone's teeth in."[8] Dowd might be just about the only person in the world to respond to *The Passion* this way. A *New York Times* reader responded to Dowd's view of the film with this incredible testimony:

> Being born and raised Jewish I would like to personally thank the writers of the *New York Times* for opening my eyes…. Maureen Dowd with her article, "Stations of the Crass" (…) came out of the movie "wanting to kick someone's teeth in." (…)
> The *NY Times* raised my curiosity enough to see *The Passion of the Christ*. I went into the theater and

---

6 Garry Wills, "God in the Hands of Angry Sinners," *The New York Times Review of Books*, Vol. 31, No. 6, April 8, 2004.

7 Reviewer "jbberber," "Reader's Reviews," *The New York Times* website, March, 24, 2004.

8 Maureen Dowd, "The Stations of the Cross," *The New York Times*, February 6, 2004.

was angry even before viewing it. As I sat and watched with my Jewish and Christian friends, a calm came over me. I felt a deep sense of love from the Jesus they knew. I was so envious. I wanted to be part of this faith that has such love and forgiveness.... I was moved to tears and was ashamed that my own people were so harshly criticizing people with such deep faith and love. My heroes in the movie were ALL JEW-ISH.... That makes me proud. Stop the hate, we must love all our brothers and sisters, Jews, Muslims, Christians... everyone. Open our hearts.

I am also proud to say that I am converting to Christianity. Jesus loves all of us, we must love him back. Thank you again. FATHER FORGIVE THEM FOR THEY KNOW NOT WHAT THEY DO.[9]

The film perhaps has its greatest influence on those who are already Christian, or who have left Christianity and are ambivalent about that decision, or who are in some way predisposed towards the Christian religion and Christian spirituality. The film also has great influence on those who are not Christian but are seeking spiritual enlightenment. The movie has generated thousands of testimonials. Many of them are posted on the Internet.

From the hundreds of testimonials this author researched, an increase in love for others seems to be one of the most common experiences produced by the film. After I saw the film for the first time I noticed that people in the theater were immediately sensitive to others and polite to a fault. When I exited my seat, for instance, a man entered the aisle that was also exiting his row. He deferred to me with exceptional politeness and gentle graciousness that is rare and I am sure was prompted by the mood

---

[9] Reviewer: "oratorium," "Inner Peace At Last," "Reader's Reviews," *The New York Times* website, March 7, 2004.

the film cast upon the audience. After the movie ended, everyone in the theater was silent—many people sat in their seats for several moments. Many were weeping. Indeed, whenever anyone did leave they exited the theater as if it were a church—quietly, with great respect for others, making an effort not to disturb the thoughts—or prayers—of others.

Simply the demeanor of those who watch *The Passion* is, in itself, evidence that this is not the usual Hollywood evening out at the movies. Many have noted that people watch this movie very differently from the usual film. One woman described *The Passion* audience: "[I]t was stunning to see how people reacted. Not a sound—no coughing, no clearing of throats, eating popcorn or getting up and stepping out to the restroom. And when it ended, people just sat there and watched the credits, then walked out with not a word spoken. Everyone was a changed person when they left the theater!"[10] One man said it very well:

> Mel Gibson's masterful rendering of *The Passion of the Christ* is not a popcorn movie. Try tossing fluffy kernels into your mouth, and your hand will freeze midway. Your mouth won't close. Your teeth won't chew. Your throat won't swallow. The very light and airy nature of this typical movie-going snack cannot compete with the gritty substance of *The Passion*.
>
> By no means a "feel good" movie, *The Passion*, nonetheless, makes you feel—in a most powerful way which works for the good. Troubles in your own life shrink in proportion as you focus on the One who redeemed us, who shed His innocent blood to pay our colossal debt which too many of us are ignorant of.[11]

---

[10] Natalie DiBella, "100 Stars for Mel," "Your Feedback on The Passion of the Christ," Christianity Today Movies, at www.christianitytoday.com, March 2, 2004.

[11] Thérèse Heckenkamp, "Take Courage, Watch the Passion," My Life After The Passion of the Christ, www.mylifeafter.com, April 9, 2004.

"Light and airy" popcorn not only can't compete with the "gritty substance" of the film, but the light and airy quality of popcorn and indeed its frivolousness is completely incongruous with the enfleshed reality of the suffering incarnate Son of God. This is why *The Passion* is not a "popcorn movie."

Audience behavior during *The Passion* is so different that the producers of the *Miracles of the Passion* documentary even filmed audience reaction with the use of night-vision cameras.[12]

The following testimonies are from the website group, My Life After *The Passion of the Christ.*

An eighteen-year-old woman, who practices Hinduism, described her experience of the movie:

> I sat amongst people of every race and heard them weep, heard them gasp and then all smile at each other when it was over. I ask each and everyone of you to go out and see this movie.... Brace yourselves for violence, expect many tears. I hope you come out of the theater and see through the obscure and false reality that has been imposed upon you by hatred, jealousy, greed and tension and become truly human again. Forgive each other.... Love each other. "You are my friends and the greatest love a person can have for his friends is to give his life for them"—Jesus Christ.[13]

A young man from Pakistan who professed to be Muslim expressed a similar experience:

> I am a Muslim and I have watched this movie at least twelve times. I am a Muslim, but that doesn't mean

---

[12] "Pax Premiers TV Special About 'Miracles of the Passion' for May Sweeps," PRWeb, www.emediawire.com, May 19, 2004.

[13] Nesha Rampersad, "A Hindu's Perspective," My Life After The Passion of the Christ, www.mylifeafter.com, March 7, 2004.

that I don't believe in Jesus. I remember each and every word of Jesus [in the film] and I am trying to improve myself by helping my brothers and sisters in the world as Jesus himself has said: "You have heard it— love those who love you and hate your enemy, but I say love those who don't love you and pray for your enemy." I am not a Christian, but I love and respect Jesus from the bottom of my heart.[14]

A 41-year-old woman who lives in Bangkok thanked Mel Gibson for making *The Passion* saying that she would never be the same again: "I will never read the Scriptures about the crucifixion in the same way ever again. I will never hate anybody ever again."[15] A 37-year-old woman who described herself as a "stay-at-home mom" declared that the movie inspired her to "be more tolerant of others and more caring. It has helped me look into myself to be a better person."[16]

A portrait artist from Albuquerque, New Mexico, who was raised Christian but as an adult practiced eastern philosophy, provided this particularly poignant testimony:

It is said that we are saved by Jesus' death. Seeing how Jesus took on such torture—and never lost his love, his giving, his compassion—moved me to the core. If he could die with such dignity, compassion and love, then I choose to honor Him by striving to live with dignity, compassion and love.

I have given up alcohol and choose to *be* with whatever difficulties life presents. I was through the

---

[14] Salman, "A Muslim Thought on the Movie," My Life After, April 29, 2004.

[15] Nok Napatalung, "The Most Powerful Movie I Have Ever Seen...," My Life After, May 14, 2004.

[16] Lisa, No title, My Life After, March 3, 2004.

mall yesterday and I looked at all these people. Usually I look past them. It hit me that to Jesus, all of these people were so beautiful, worth dying for, as if they were His own children. I pray for the grace to see the world this way and to live in this world in the way Jesus did.[17]

Certainly one of the most common responses to *The Passion* is an increased awareness of the love of God for the individual. In a real way, this response fulfills Gibson's own intention for the movie when he stated: "My new hope is that *The Passion of the Christ* will help many more people recognize the power of His love and let Him help them to save their own lives."[18] Seeing the loving, patient, compassionate God-Man endure unspeakable tortures for the love of the human race produces this reaction.

The national newspaper *USA Today* interviewed people immediately after they viewed the movie on the day it opened, Ash Wednesday, 2004. Fifty-year-old David Walcott of Brooklyn, New York, stated, "It was a harsh reality to see the sufferings of Christ, however, it causes me to love Christ more for what he did for me and the whole world, Jews and Gentiles."[19] Another woman tells how an increased awareness of God's love affected her right away: "The first thing I learned while watching this magnificent movie is that there truly is no greater love than the one that our Father and Jesus have for us. I have experienced love on a different level and my faith has grown even more."[20]

Christ's love becomes very real for the viewer:

---

[17] Fran, "In As Buddhists, Out As Christians," My Life After, March 3, 2004.

[18] Mel Gibson, "Foreword," *The Passion*, TAN Books and Publishers, Rockford, IL, 2004.

[19] Liz Szabo, et. al., "'Passion' Provokes Strong Reactions," *USA Today*, February, 26, 2004.

[20] Ana Nenadic, "No Greater Love," Christianity Today Movies, April 19, 2004.

Watching *The Passion of the Christ* has made Christ's love very real to me. Watching this movie, I could barely breathe. I was terrified, shocked and awed. All I could think about was how ridiculous my little problems are, and how I put too much focus on them. I don't think I had a true understanding of the extent of Christ's love for us until I saw this movie. Walking out of the theater my arms, legs and voice were shaking. I have had a lump in my throat and been brought to tears many times over the last week just thinking about it, and I have re-read all four Gospels regarding the betrayal through crucifixion, and his love for us really became real for me.[21]

The New York Times posted on its website almost four hundred "readers reviews" of *The Passion*. The paper specifically invited audience reaction to the movie's treatment of the Jews and its violence. The vast majority of the responses submitted to the *Times* were amazingly positive. The comment below reflects most of the readers' sentiments:

I thought this movie would be too much for me graphically from all I read. That was far from the truth. After seeing this movie I have never been moved more than to see what Jesus did for me; no one has ever loved me more than this.

I have never cried in a movie being the strong emotional man that I am... but I had tears streaming down my face. When the movie ended I left with peace in my heart and contemplation in my mind [22]

---

[21] Stacy Ployhar, "Shock and Awe," Christianity Today Movies, March, 10, 2004.

[22] Reviewer: "maphere," "Ride of Your Life," "Reader's Reviews," *The New York Times* website, March 9, 2004.

Justin, a railroad signalman was inspired to get his "spiritual life back on track." With tears welling up in his eyes he wrote, "…because even with all the stupid and mean things I have done in my life, Jesus will still forgive me and wrap me in his love. That is a very powerful feeling. I wish I could thank Mel Gibson personally for the awakening I had today. I know that I can only become a better person, a more loving Father, a more compassionate Husband and a more dedicated Christian because of this movie."[23]

Increased Prayer and Bible Reading

A special dimension of the conversion experience prompted by *The Passion of the Christ* is that many people have a renewed interest in prayer, in reciting the rosary and reading Scripture. A woman from Livermore, California, said that after viewing the film she was prompted to pray the rosary and meditate on Christ's Passion for the first time in fifteen years. Furthermore, raised a Catholic, she had left the Church to become a Protestant but states that through the movie God spoke to her heart and she was inspired to return to the Catholic faith.[24] Another woman, who was not particularly religious, said "I feel like my life will never be the same…. This movie really hit me in the heart. Now I read the Bible every night. I really let Jesus into my heart. I now realize I can go through anything and do anything."[25]

A man raised as a Conservative Jew, but who converted to Christianity in 1973 described how *The Passion* helped deepen

---

[23] Justin, No title, My Life After, March 7, 2004.

[24] Janice Lima, "I Prayed the Rosary," Ibid., May 20, 2004.

[25] Maria, "My Opened Eyes," Ibid., March 22, 2004.

his understanding of the Messianic Seders he had hosted over the years:

> Mary, the mother of Jesus, has a reaction right when they are arresting Jesus. She gets up from her bed and says, "Why is this night different from all other nights?" Mary recognized that her son was about to take on the role of the Passover Lamb. I saw many other connections related to the Lord's Supper (His last Passover Seder) and the scenes surrounding the cross (especially because I have been privileged to present Messianic Seders the last 26 years). This movie has impacted forever how I will present my own Seder ceremonies this season and in seasons to come.[26]

Michael Hale, a Protestant pastor for thirty years, explains how *The Passion* will forever affect his preaching: "I will never preach the cross again without thinking about the realistic portrayal in *The Passion*. I felt like I had been to Calvary when I left the showing."[27]

One of the most significant consequences of *The Passion* is the way it has increased appreciation for the Sacrament of the Eucharist—both for Catholics and Protestants. A gentleman, aged thirty-five, from South Carolina stated, "One thing that really changed in my life after seeing the film is my view of Communion. The breaking of the bread and the wine really takes on a whole new meaning in my life now. I really did not give much thought to it. But since seeing this film and how Jesus suffered and gave his life for me, the sacrament of Communion really hits home."[28]

---

[26] Stan Kellner, "Messianic Message," Christianity Today Movies, March 10, 2004.

[27] Michael Hale, "I've Been to Calvary," Ibid., March 10, 2004.

[28] Jim, "Communion," My Life After, April 20, 2004.

Even Catholics testify that their appreciation for Holy Communion and the Mass increased. A woman from Atlanta, Georgia, who is a devout Catholic, said, "I saw the movie the day before it opened and, being Catholic, attended Mass on Ash Wednesday and a Stations of the Cross meditation. Receiving Communion at Mass was almost a whole new experience. Several times during Mass I felt moved to tears. During the Stations meditation I felt much more in touch with what actually happened. The words spoken were much more meaningful."[29]

Even a priest, someone who has dedicated his whole life to the Catholic liturgy, expressed: "I will not celebrate Mass the same after this movie, which reflects many important aspects of our Catholic faith: the value of Jesus' blood, the role of Mary in the Passion, the importance of the human life of Jesus, etc."[30]

And finally, a viewer put together Isaiah 53 and the significance of Communion: "The phrase, 'by his stripes we are healed' now has true meaning for me. When I take Communion next time, I will truly understand how [Jesus] suffered and died for me and all of us."[31]

Taking the Passion Personally

Another remarkable response to this film is the way in which many people see themselves in the movie. Many especially identify with Pontius Pilate and the Roman soldiers who are responsible for the torture Jesus endures. This is a very spiritual experience for these viewers as they see their own sinfulness in these characters.

---

[29] Lisa, No title, My Life After, March 3, 2004.

[30] Fr. Roberto Mena, S.T., "The Passion of a Priest," Christianity Today Movies, March 10, 2004.

[31] L. Rutkowski, "New Look on Communion," Ibid., March 2, 2004.

Each of us enters this film where it begins—with Jesus, alone, in the Garden of Gethsemane. I immediately saw… myself… sound asleep while my Lord and Savior bled torment. How long I wondered have I been napping while our rancid culture seduces our young!

In the scene depicting Christ's betrayal, I heard myself think: "How many times have I sold you out, O Lord—exchanging the priceless treasure of your truth for material gain? (…) When Jesus is scourged, a scene that takes roughly two millennia to end, I asked, "Lord, was that spiked cord which lashed your back not my tongue and why is it I can't stop judging, stop criticizing, stop… inflicting?"

When Christ falls under the weight of the cross: "Was it I, Lord, who took you down? Have I not also, conspired to remove you from the public square? Have I not, also, been complicit in marginalizing your voice in the affairs of modern man?"

When the Cyrenean, a Jew, was pressed into service in order that Christ might not die before He can be killed, I could not but ask: "How many times have I failed to accept, much less embrace, the mystery, indeed, the gift, of suffering in my life?"[32]

One commentator on *The Passion* saw herself in Pontius Pilate:

In the movie's Pilate, I saw myself luxuriating in my wealth while others went hungry. I saw myself reflecting on philosophy while those who worked for me whipped Jesus. I saw myself afraid of Caesar,

---

[32] Brian J. Gail, *"The Passion of the Christ*—A Reflection," *Star* Magazine, March/April 2004.

caught between the distant but powerful government and my own better impulses. There I was the anti-war liberal good girl, washing my hands of moral responsibility, while soldiers bled and Iraqis burned. My fear, my philosophical reflection, and my self-awareness don't absolve me any more than they did Pilate. My hands aren't clean.[33]

The movie arouses a deep sense of personal responsibility for the sufferings of Christ.

"I" put those stripes, bruises, nail holes on him. I could no longer point a finger at anyone else, I had to take the blame. The guilt I felt for what my sin had done to a perfect, sinless lamb was overwhelming.[34]

The blood will catch your attention, but it is the angry crowd, the frightened disciples running away, the Romans who beat him and laughed, and the Jewish leaders who judge, the mocking/jeering faces that may have the deeper effect. I see myself in that crowd, and know I have hurt Jesus many times with my sin. The ugliness will make you sad; it made me weep.[35]

[The movie] is about what Jesus has done for the whole world. He paid the price. Our sin whipped every inch of his sinless body. Our hatefulness and wickedness drove the spikes through his hands and his feet. Our self-centeredness raised the cross, and our darkness snuffed out the Light of the World... but not for long. After watching the movie, an Iranian friend,

---

[33] Linda Dickey, "I Am Pontius Pilate," in Godspy, Faith at the Edge, www.godspy.com, March 1, 2004.

[34] Veronica Clark, "I Take the Blame," Christianity Today Movies, March 1, 2004.

[35] Amelia Palmer, "A Ticket Back In Time," Ibid., March 10, 2004.

whom I had the privilege of baptizing several years ago, said in her beautiful accent, "I love him all the more, I love him all the more."[36]

It made me look at my own life and made me think that all those beatings he took was for me and my sins. I will never be the same again.[37]

It is extremely interesting to note how even the veteran film critic Roger Ebert talked about *The Passion*. Ebert assured his readers, in his February 25, 2004 review, that he was "no longer religious in the sense that a long ago altar boy thought he should be." However, Ebert said that when, as an altar boy, he assisted at the "Stations of the Cross this was not necessarily a deep religious experience":

Christ suffered, Christ died, Christ rose again, we were redeemed and let's hope we can get home on time to watch the Illinois basketball game on TV. What Gibson has provided for me, for the first time in my life, is a visceral idea of what the Passion consisted of.[38]

His review has a hint of a confession of faith. When he defines the meaning of the word "passion" for instance, Ebert says the word includes "Christ's love for mankind, which made him willing to suffer and die *for us*" (emphasis added). In describing Gibson's intent for the film, Ebert says he wanted to "make graphic and inescapable the price that Jesus paid (…) when he died *for our sins*" (emphasis added). Jesus died *for us*—

---

[36] Reverend Steven S. Bryant, "I Love Him All the More," Ibid., February 26, 2004.

[37] Cheri Lee Testa, "I'll Never Be the Same," Christianity Today Movies, February 26, 2004.

[38] Roger Ebert, "The Passion of the Christ," *Chicago Sun-Times*, February 24, 2004.

died *for our sins*. These are faith-based statements, declarative of faith. If Ebert wanted to sound neutral or distance himself from the Christian religion he would have said something like "according to Christianity, Jesus died for the sins of the human race." When Ebert uses the word "us"—this is a personal word and he includes himself, as well as the whole world, in the circle of "us" for whom Christ died.

Confessing Criminals

Many critics of *The Passion* predicted that the movie's depiction of the Jews would unleash a new wave of anti-Semitism and crimes against the Jews. Indeed, the very opposite occurred after the film opened in theaters nationwide. The movie provoked remorse in at least four criminals, one of whom had even committed a murder. These criminals turned themselves in to the police and confessed to their crimes.

The first criminal to turn himself over to authorities was 21-year-old Dan Leach of Rosenberg, Texas. On January 19, 2004, Leach's girlfriend, Ashley Wilson, was found hanging from her bedpost. Her death was ruled a suicide. In March 2004, after watching *The Passion*, Leach "stood in front of his church congregation and said that he had done something wrong" as reported by the *Fort Bend/Southwest Sun* in Houston. Leach then went home and in front of his minister, church elders and parents confessed that he had murdered Ashley.[39] Leach killed his girlfriend because she was pregnant and he did not want to care for the baby. He made her death look like a suicide from information gained on TV detective shows. Jeanne Gage, a public information officer for the Fort Bend County Sheriff's Office stated

---

[39] "Film Inspires Wave of Crime Confessions," World Net Daily, www.worldnetdaily.com, March 31, 2004.

that Leach "cited the film as one of the reasons for turning himself in."[40] Ashley's mother, Renee Coulter felt a sense of relief at Leach's confession as she told the *Sun*: "In my heart I knew she did not kill herself, and it is confirmed that I knew my daughter, and she wouldn't have done this."[41]

Two robbers also confessed to their crimes: 20-year-old Turner Lee Bingham of Mesa, Arizona, and Florida bank robber, James Anderson, who had been a fugitive for more than two years.

Bingham had committed a series of robberies. Immediately after taking eighty dollars from the cash register of a Mesa store he apologized to police for his action and confessed to the other burglaries. Bingham said that he had seen *The Passion* with his mother and felt guilty.[42]

Anderson had stolen 25,000 dollars from a Palm Beach Gardens bank in December 2001. He told police that he came clean about his crime after watching *The Passion*. Paul Miller, sheriff's office spokesman, stated that Anderson said, "I saw *The Passion* and that made my decision." Miller added that Anderson urged him to see the movie too.[43]

Perhaps the most ironic confession was that of convicted murderer and Neo-Nazi leader Johnny Olsen in Oslo, Norway. Instead of Christians bashing Jews, *The Passion of the Christ* prompted a Jew-hater to turn himself over to the police. Olsen had already served twelve years in prison for the slayings of two youths in 1981.

> On Saturday evening [March 27, 2004] one of Norway's most feared men, walked into the offices of the Dagbladet and confessed to two bombings of

---

[40] Tim Drake, "Passion Confessions," *National Catholic Register*, April 11-17, 2004.
[41] "Film," World Net Daily.
[42] Ibid.
[43] Ibid.

Oslo's Blitz House, a self-styled 'counter-cultural' center that is a gathering spot for young left-wing radicals…. Olsen said that he had decided to confess after watching *The Passion of the Christ*. He said it was the film that made him realize that he had to show his hand. "He has been preoccupied with Christianity, guilt, punishment, atonement, suffering and conversion during the ten years I have known him," said Olsen's lawyer Fridtjof Feydt. "It has been a long process but the Jesus film made the difference. Now he shows true regret and wants to make amends," Feydt said.[44]

After I had heard about these confessions I began to watch *The Passion* attentive to what part of the film might actually move criminals to confess their crimes. I think it might very well be the Good Thief's own heartfelt cry from the cross: "We are getting what we deserve, but this man is innocent!" The criminal very well can see himself in the place of Dismas—the thief who confessed his own guilt, but also confessed his faith in Christ—and Jesus turned to him and said, "This day you shall be with me in Paradise" (Luke 23:43).

The Protestant Perspective

The Passion of the Christ is a movie filled with Catholic imagery, Catholic theology, Catholic devotional perspectives and was made by a self-professed traditionalist Catholic. Nonetheless, millions of Protestant believers have embraced this movie

---

[44] Karin Bohm-Pedersen, "Confessed After Seeing 'Passion'," Aftenposten, www.aftenposten.com, March 28, 2004.

and found it at least spiritually edifying, if not indeed spiritually life-changing.

Among Protestant denominations, Evangelical Christians have been the most vocally supportive of Gibson's film. However, many other mainline Protestant leaders and churches praised the movie and encouraged Christians to see it. The United Theological Seminary of the United Methodist Church posted a full study guide to *The Passion* to aid church members to reflect on the movie. Tyron Inbody, Professor of Theology at the seminary, composed a very detailed and thoughtful analysis of the film. While he had some theological reservations, Inbody's critique was extremely positive.[45]

Reverend Eric C. Shafer, director of the department of Communications for the Evangelical Lutheran Church of America, expressed some reservations about the film, but nonetheless saw *The Passion* as an opportunity for "outreach, education and dialog."[46]

President of the American Anglican Council, Canon David C. Anderson highly praised the film. He credited Gibson for causing the Stations to come alive for him.[47]

Mel Gibson was surprised by the enthusiastic support his movie received from non-Catholics, particularly from Protestant Evangelicals. He stated, "I've been actually amazed at the way I would say the evangelical audience has—hands down—responded to this film more than any other Christian group." He

---

[45] Thomas Inbody, "A Theologian's Analysis of the Movie Maker as Theologian: Mel Gibson's 'The Passion of the Christ'," Study Guides and Resources for "The Passion of the Christ" Film, United Theological Seminary, www.united.edu.

[46] Reverend Eric C. Shafer, "'The Passion of the Christ' (The Gospels Meet 'Ben Hur' Meets 'Braveheart'," Evangelical Lutheran Church in America, Communication Resources, www.elca.com, January 23, 2004.

[47] Reverend Canon David C. Anderson, "AAC President Comments on Mel Gibson's 'The Passion of the Christ'," American Anglican Council, www.americananglican.com, February 27, 2004.

was particularly surprised because the movie is very Marian. He admits that, "The way the film displays [Mary] has been kind of an eye-opener for evangelicals who don't usually look at that aspect."[48]

Billy Graham, America's most well-known evangelist, stated that *The Passion* moved him to tears and doubted "there has ever been a more graphic and moving presentation of Jesus' death and resurrection...." He praised the movie for its fidelity to Scripture and for showing "that we are all responsible for Jesus' death because we have all sinned."[49] His son Franklin Graham also stated, "Whatever your perspective, if you watch Mel Gibson's new movie *The Passion of the Christ* you will never look at the cross the same way again. Those who are perishing without Christ will have to confront their own foolishness. And those of us who are saved will be powerfully challenged to grow in our faith and reach out to others."[50] James Dobson, who heads Focus on the Family and is also a very popular Protestant leader, had nothing but high praise for *The Passion*. He stated, "It isn't often that I find myself speaking favorably about a modern movie, but there is a film being released this month that I believe is among the most powerful ever made. I am talking about *The Passion of the Christ....* I can say that in addition to being faithful to the biblical account, it is easily the most heart-wrenching, powerful portrayal of Christ's sufferings that I have ever seen."[51]

Several other Protestant leaders and organizations endorsed the movie such as Jack Graham, President of the Southern Bap-

---

[48] David Neff, "Mel, Mary and Mothers," *Christianity Today*, March 2004.

[49] "Mel Gibson Gives Billy Graham Special Screening of 'The Passion'," Baptist Press, www.bpnews.net, December 3, 2004.

[50] Franklin Graham, "The Point of 'The Passion'," *Decision* Magazine, March 2004, Billy Graham Evangelistic Association, www.billygraham.org.

[51] James Dobson, "The Greatest Story Ever Told," Focus on the Family, www.family.org, February 2004.

tist Convention; Peter Crouch of Trinity Broadcasting Network; Greg Laurie, Harvest Crusades; Roger Cross, president of Youth for Christ/USA; Paul Cedar, Chairman and CEO of Mission America Coalition; Max Lucado, a pastor and best-selling author; Chuck Colson, Tim LaHaye, Jerry Falwell, Pat Boone, Pat Robertson, author Lee Strobel, Pastor Bill Hybels, and Cal Thomas. The Protestant group, Campus Crusade for Christ, saw the movie as "an evangelistic opportunity that is unlikely to be repeated in our lifetime."[52] This was echoed by Brian Bloomberg, Vice President and Chief Development Officer for Promise Keepers, who said the Gibson film "may be the next great evangelism tool of our time."[53]

Why have so many Protestants warmed up to an overtly Catholic movie? One explanation is that some Protestants just might not be aware of how Catholic the movie is. They are not keyed in to the theological imagery. One Protestant viewer of the film stated, "I highly doubt that the florid ramblings of a nun of the Counter-Reformation would produce a version of Christ's Passion that would be so palatable to American Evangelicals."[54] *Newsweek*'s contributing editor Kenneth Woodward wondered how a movie so steeped in Catholic imagery could appeal to evangelical Protestants. He noted that evangelicals are the heirs "to an iconoclastic tradition that produced the 'stripping of altars'... and removed Christ's body from the cross.... For evangelicals, the symbols are all in sermon and song: verbal icons. It's a different sensibility."[55] Woodward expected evangelicals to be shocked by what they saw in *The Passion*.

---

[52] Campus Crusade, www.christianity.ca/church/outreach/2004.

[53] Brian Bloomberg, Promise Keepers at www.WarriorsofChristJesus@groups.msn.com.

[54] Reader's response to Frank Rich, *Free Republic*, www.freerepublic.com, August 1, 2003.

[55] Kenneth Woodward, "Do You Recognize This Jesus," *The New York Times*, February 25, 2003.

Certainly one of the reasons the Gibson film appeals to Protestants is that, despite its huge dependence on the *Dolorous Passion* by Anne Catherine Emmerich, most of what is depicted on the screen is solidly biblical. Protestants find their own doctrine affirmed in the film: Jesus is the divine Son of God, the source of all human redemption who, because of His love for mankind, endured the pain of the cross. A *Christianity Today* article by David Neff provided several explanations why *The Passion* is so popular among Protestant audiences. Neff notes that the film was shaped by a devout Roman Catholic, "But evangelicals have not found that a problem because, overall, the theology of the film articulates powerful themes that have been important to all classical Christians."[56] First of all, *The Passion*, from the very start of the film, is about the cosmic battle between good and evil, "between God and the Devil." Moreover, as Gibson told an audience at Willow Creek Church in Illinois, the Devil in his movie, "takes on the form of beauty. It is almost beautiful. It is the great aper of God. But the mask is askew; there's always something wrong. Evil masquerades, but if your antennae are up, you'll detect it." This idea reflects St. Paul's theology. He taught that "Satan masquerades as an angel of light" (2 Corinthians 11:14). Protestants can identify with this.

The Passion also emphasizes the reality of personal sin. Sin is not simply social. Each individual is guilty before God. This is a theme Protestants understand. However, this idea is also in Emmerich, as Neff notes: "The visionary Emmerich wrote: 'Among the sins which Jesus took upon himself, I saw also my own; and a stream, in which I distinctly beheld each of my faults, appeared to flow towards me out of the temptations with which he was encircled.'"[57] Not only is there a strong sense of personal sin in the movie, but also a strong sense of personal

---

[56] David Neff, "The Passion of Mel Gibson," *Christianity Today*, March 2004.
[57] Ibid.

salvation.[58] The devout Christian can see the great price Christ paid to win the human race back to the Father. The movie also aids Protestant "cross-centered" devotion. Neff observes that many Protestants are discovering meditation in which they place themselves into the biblical scene—the sort of mental prayer that Catholics have practiced for centuries.[59] Finally, *The Passion* appeals to Protestants because it emphasizes the need for blood sacrifice:

> "The enormity of blood sacrifice," as he put it, is important to Gibson. Unlike liberal Christians (both Catholic and Protestant) who deny the importance of the shedding of blood in the Atonement, Gibson grasps firmly the sacred symbol of blood and splatters the audiences' sensibilities with it. Never one to run from a compelling symbol, Gibson presents the truth of Leviticus 17:11 in all its power: "The life of the flesh is in its blood; and I have given it for you upon the altar to make atonement for your souls; for it is the blood that makes atonement, by reason of the life."[60]

Of course, while huge numbers of Protestants love *The Passion*, there is a small but committed minority, of mostly Evangelical Protestants, who despise the film and even accuse it of being a product of Satan. Their primary complaint is that *The Passion* is not true to the Gospels and is obsessed with Mary. As one pastor stated: "They should have named the film *The Passion of Jesus and Mary*. The film is wrought with an unbiblical fixation on Mary, the mother of Jesus. What's even more disturbing and disgusting is the reason for the fixation. Mel Gibson clearly presents Mary as the co-redemptrix... a belief and teach-

---

58 Ibid.

59 Ibid.

60 Ibid.

ing found in Roman Catholicism, which is contrary to Scripture. Because of this, Mary, who is mentioned only once in the Bible during the time frame Gibson's film covers, is the focus of Gibson's cameras nearly as much as Jesus.... When you read the book of Acts and any of the epistles of the New Testament, you see they preached Christ and him crucified—not Christ and Mary.... When you truly see the beauty of this, you see how abhorrent Gibson's film is."[61]

The Marian theological themes of *The Passion* that some Protestants find so disgusting are the very images that make many Catholics fall in love with the movie. Consider these nearly absolutely opposite observations:

> It shocks me that *The Passion* is hailed by many fundamentalist Christian groups as a soul-winning tool and a soul-stirring movie.... Did no one else notice that Mary was the co-star of this movie as she is the "co-star" in the Catholic Church? It showed her somehow linked with Jesus throughout the movie as if they had a bond akin to a psychic "mind-meld"—like the scene in which she is able to locate him as he hung in chains in the prison below.
>
> And what a frightening picture at the end as Christ's lifeless body was removed from the cross and placed into her arms. Did the camera stay fixed on him? No. It focuses on Mary's knowing smile, as if the fate of the world rested on HER, not in Christ.... This movie was not inspired by God, but rather by Satan, as he blinds us to the truth and causes us to accept unscriptural beliefs as we head into the end times.[62]

---

[61] Matt Trewhella, "The Passion of the Christ or the Emperor's New Clothes," www.mercyseat.net, February 24, 2004.

[62] Bonnie Wykoff, "Caught Up In the Hype?", Christianity Today Movies, www.christianitytoday.com, March 18, 2004.

A Catholic saw something completely different (and not a smiling Mary at all at the end of the film!):

> Mel Gibson has truly created an artistic masterpiece. Even more importantly, he has fashioned a cinematic tribute to the glory and truth of Catholicism.... From its depiction of the Blessed Mother's prominent role in the narrative (comforting St. Peter and St. Mary Magdalen as their "mother") viscerally experiencing the suffering of Our Lord, confronting Satan on the Via Dolorosa, to its masterful juxtaposition of the Eucharistic Sacrifice of the Last Supper with that of Our Lord's Sacrifice on Calvary, *The Passion* boldly asserts its Catholic sensibility as no other film has for the last forty years.[63]

Perhaps the most thorough critique of *The Passion* critical of its non-biblical perspectives came from Terry Watkins of Dial-the-Truth-Ministries. Watkins posted his extensive commentary on the Internet. Called "The Poison in the Passion Movie," it is hard to imagine a better researched and detailed critique of what's "wrong" with the Gibson film from a Protestant point of view. Watkins deserves praise for his painstaking research of Emmerich's *Dolorous Passion*. His lengthy analysis of the film includes a section that matches nearly every scene in the Gibson film with the scenes described in Emmerich's writings. This is a critic of the movie who really did his homework!

Besides the fact that *The Passion* is based on the visions of a nun, whom Watkins describes as "a very spiritually disturbed lady," he hates the movie for a number of other reasons:

1. He believes that, contrary to the warnings of Scripture, the movie "adds" to the Word of God.

---

[63] Robert Pickard, "Catholic Sensibilities," Ibid., March 10, 2004.

2. The movie must be condemned, in principle, because it depends upon Catholic devotions, in particular, the Stations of the Cross, which again contain elements that are not found in the Bible—most notably Veronica wiping the face of Jesus.
3. He says the movie exalts the Catholic liturgy of the Mass—and Latin is used in the film for this purpose.
4. Viewers should beware of allowing their minds to be infected with images of false doctrine.
5. The violence of the movie and its "R" rating make it unsuitable for children, contrary to Christ's teaching, "Suffer little children to come unto me, and forbid them not: for such is the kingdom of God" (Luke 18:16).
6. Watkins opposes the idea of any man portraying the Lord as he stated, "I find it very degrading and irreverent for anyone to 'play' or 'act' as the person of the Lord Jesus Christ. I believe there are some things a Christian should not 'play' with. I believe there are some things that are simply too sacred and too glorious for man to 'touch.' And the person of Our Lord Jesus Christ is one of these."[64]

It is very ironic that often those who oppose *The Passion* do, in fact, understand its imagery and themes. Watkins, for instance, more than nearly any other critic or even supporter of the movie, sees each Station of the Cross in the film. He sees very clearly the ritual dimension of the movie: "*The Passion* is the Catholic ritual 'The Stations of the Cross' in action.... It is the Catholic 'Stations of the Cross' carried out on film."[65] He also understands the theological importance of the use of foreign languages in the film, especially Latin. Another commen-

---

[64] Terry Watkins, "The Poison in the Passion Movie," Dial-the-Truth-Ministries, at www.av1611.org/Passion/passion.html.

[65] Ibid.

tator quoted by Watkins states, "This film, for its author is a Mass: let it be, then, in an obscure language [Latin], as it was for so many centuries."[66] He criticized the movie for its emphasis on the material suffering of Christ because "it speaks to the flesh." But this is exactly the point—the movie takes the Incarnation of God seriously. Watkins thinks the suffering of Christ is not realistic in the movie. According to him, Jesus' sufferings were far worse than what is depicted in the movie. Watkins quotes Isaiah 52:14: "[H]is visage was so marred more than any other man, and his form more than the sons of men." Yet, Watkins will not credit Gibson for indeed showing the marred visage of Christ. Finally, Watkins criticized the movie for its obsession with the blood of Jesus, and moviegoers for allowing themselves to be attracted by this aspect of the film. As the movie is not even in a language viewers understand, Watkins stated, "The only thing they understand is the blood."[67] But again this is precisely the theological point Gibson wishes to make. The blood of Christ saves the human race, not His teachings *per se*, or His miracles *per se*—but His sacrifice borne in love. Watkins even quotes the words of a song to demonstrate the spiritual inadequacies of the film.

> Oh the shame of it
> My sins crucified him that day
> My sins were to blame
> Forgive, Lord, I pray
> I'll live so the world can know
> I love Him
> For nailing my sins to the cross.[68]

And many viewers see *The Passion* exactly this way.

---

[66] Ibid.

[67] Ibid.

[68] Ibid.

Theologizing

Unlike any other religious movie, *The Passion of the Christ* has provoked countless theological discussions all over the world. This is one of the most important fruits of this film. The movie provokes healthy and intense theological discussion and debate. The movie has great power to stir the theological imagination. The resulting conversations, many of which have taken place on numerous Internet blogs, are exciting and provocative. This theological quest, prompted by the movie, is filled with joy and pleasure—the kind of spiritual pleasure of the soul that comes from the desire to understand the Christian faith and deepen one's love for Jesus.

It is also significant that these discussions are engaged in by ordinary laymen and are not the special privileged dialogue of the professional theologian. Truly, *The Passion* has provided the "man on the street" with the opportunity to seriously ponder and talk about the meaning of the Christian faith.

Many of these "amateur theologians" come up with refreshing and startling insights into the themes and images of the Gibson film.

I attended a discussion group on the movie at my parish church. We discussed the meaning of the very disturbing image of the thief whose eye is poked out by a raven. Many reviewers of the movie dismiss this image as simply Gibson's way of telling the audience that God is wrathful towards those who mock His Son. However, the image means something else altogether. One parishioner suggested that the key to this image might lie in Christ's parable of the sower and the seed. This parable is about the Word of God that is sown among various kinds of people represented by different kinds of ground. The farmer, who represents God, sows his seed and some "fell on the footpath where it was walked on and birds of the air ate it up." Jesus explained, "Those on the footpath are people who hear, but the

Devil comes and takes the word out of their hearts lest they believe and be saved" (Luke 8:5-12). The thief on the cross is in the very presence of the suffering Lord, hears His prayers, watches Him die, yet he remains on the side of the Devil. He is "eaten up by the birds of the air." This is a good example of someone who ponders the meaning of *The Passion* and probes the spiritual dimension of the images.

An informal review of the movie appeared on the website "Grammy and PapaJoe's Blog" which describes itself as "The Latest on Life Arlington Eastland and Beyond." Here are some theological conclusions of this review:

> I asked my daughter-in-law's father if he saw the fly larva (maggot) protruding and wiggling just slightly out of Rosalinda's nose [the actress who played Satan] during the prayers in the Garden sequence. You know that Satan represented death, just from seeing the maggot ever so briefly....
>
> A talk show host had described how you could see Jesus' ribs. I made sure I watched and yes at one point, I did see two ribs.* Seeing the ribs made me mentally look back to the creation of the man Adam (through Adam there is death), and the woman from Adam's rib. But through Christ there is life....
>
> When the Centurion pierced His side and blood and water came forth, it showed him kneeling and the WATER that spewed from His side did not look bloody, it looked as if it were cleansing his face. Hence, the blood of Christ cleansing us from our sins....
>
> The Romans were shown standing on top of the back of the cross hammering the points down, add-

---

* Two ribs are visible on Christ's left side as He lies on the pavement when the scourging is over.

ing their weight to the cross. This hurt me more than the flogging and even the piercing. At that point I could see the weight of my sin on Jesus, more than anywhere else during the depiction.[69]

In the article "Two Zen Men and a Christian at *The Passion*" a young Christian gentleman tells the story of how he invited his two non-Christian friends to the movie and their reactions to it. Both friends practiced Eastern meditation in the Buddhist tradition.

After the movie they all went to a restaurant. The two Buddhists began to ask questions about the movie. A very interesting discussion took place on the nature of Christ and His mission. The two Buddhists were impressed that Jesus lived the teaching that He preached. They saw the complete unity, the total integrity of the "man" and His message.

One of the friends remarked, "Jesus, what he preached, his code, it was just exactly who he was. There was no difference."

This insight led to the final conclusion that the Christian religion (unlike Buddhism and Hinduism, etc.) is not a philosophy, or a message, but a *person*. Indeed, that unlike other religions, Jesus *the person* is central to the faith—*He is the faith*.

> We talked about the teachings of the great Zen master, Fukushima Roshi, under whom Gene studies and practices. Gene wanted to know if Christianity is a philosophy, or a religion, or a Church. Roshi says Zen is a religion. I told Gene that Christianity is a person, and the person is that guy who crawled up onto the cross.[70]

---

[69] "The Passion of the Christ Grammy Review/as asked of Chip," Grammy and Papa Joe's Blog, www.grammyandpapajoe.blogspot.com, March 1, 2004.

[70] Dave Sloan, "Two Zen Men and a Christian at The Passion," Godspy, www.godspy.com, February 27, 2004.

Through *The Passion* two practitioners of Eastern religion were introduced to the essence of Christianity and began to think about it.

One viewer of the film provided insight into Jesus' prayer in the garden:

> *The Passion of the Christ* begins with Jesus' agonizing prayer in the Garden of Gethsemane—one in which he quotes from Psalm 31: "In you, O Lord, I have taken refuge.... Free me from the trap that is set for me." Psalm 31 is one of the "imprecatory" psalms, or psalms of rage, where David holds nothing back: "Let the wicked be put to shame and lie silent in the grave" (Psalm 31:17). While the Gospels don't say that Jesus quoted this psalm in the Garden, he clearly did so on the cross: "Into your hands I commit my spirit" (31:5). So did Jesus have all of Psalm 31 in mind—with David's plea for vengeance—or just the more palatable verses? Was [Jesus] praying the "prayer of revenge"? Jesus may well have had to go through the whole forgiveness process, just as the rest of us do—beginning with acknowledging the desire for vindication. I think it makes sense that Jesus prayed the entire Psalm because all of it together represents the forgiveness process, not just the final plea for mercy on behalf of one's offenders.[71]

Occasionally the "amateur theologians" will come up with an explanation for a particular image that even outdoes Mel Gibson. This was the case, for instance, with Satan and the demon child. Gibson explained, "Again, it's evil distorting what is

---

[71] Doug Schmidt, author of *Prayer of Revenge: Forgiveness in the Face of Injustice,* "A Prayer of Revenge," Christianity Today Movies, www.christianitytoday.com, March 10, 2004.

good. What is more tender and beautiful than a mother and a child? So the devil takes that and distorts it just a bit. Instead of a normal mother and child you have an androgynous figure holding a 40-year-old 'baby' with hair on his back. It is weird, it is shocking, just like turning Jesus over to continue scourging him on his chest is shocking... which is the exact moment when this appearance of the devil and the baby takes place."[72]

An observer of the film wasn't satisfied with Gibson's explanation:

> Mel Gibson's explanation about the "baby" in Satan's arms was a little disappointing. It seemed to me the symbolism didn't go far enough. I immediately saw the baby as the anti-Christ. The "baby" sees Jesus suffering and smirks, enjoying the sensuality of the evil moment. The anti-Christ would most enjoy the destruction of Christ.[73]

A discussion group sponsored by the Legionaries of Christ, a Catholic order of priests, resulted in this observation—without any reference to Emmerich or Mary of Agreda:

> There is a scene at the crucifixion where Mary Magdalen is the only one who sees a miracle happen. It is a very quick scene and it happens when she is on her knees.... Jesus has been nailed to the cross and the Romans are turning it over. You expect Jesus to smash His face into the ground when the cross falls over but it does not happen. Instead what you see is the Magdalen looking up to see that the cross is floating above the ground. She is the only one to see that Jesus

---

[72] Mark Moring, "What's Up With the Ugly Baby?," Ibid., March 1, 2004.
[73] Lucille Yuen, "More on the Ugly Baby," Ibid., March 10, 2004.

is floating a few inches above the ground the entire time that they are hammering the nails on the back of the cross to secure them. It is a representation of God still in control of the whole crucifixion process.[74]

The movie also sparked some interesting theological discussions between Catholics and Protestants. In a chat room of the website "Spero," dedicated to Protestant and Catholic dialogue, a debate took place on whether viewers of the Gibson film commit the sin of idolatry. The Protestant raised the question: If people pray because of the images in the movie, isn't this basically the same thing as Catholics who pray in front of statues and paintings? The Catholic party responded, "[D]o you think the evangelicals were praying TO the images, or to God? Like the reviewer reported, he wanted to keep repeating, 'I'm sorry, Jesus…' [when he saw the images on the screen]. Do you think he was worshiping graven images?"[75]

The Christian with his Zen friends even theologized on how one should attend the film. He said, don't go alone:

> Jesus' Passion is hard to bear and you'll need help. A big part of the movie is simply the largely wordless experience of Mary, John and Mary Magdalen bearing it together. Even Jesus couldn't bear his cross alone, as the compelling participation of Simon of Cyrene proves…. It's hard to watch [Jesus] being lifted up to suffocate and die there. In the end though, we do have to watch. Because he is being crucified around us even now. He is being starved, scourged, beaten, murdered, racked with disease and neglect,

---

[74] "Symbolism in the Passion Movie," notes taken at a group discussion with a Legionaries of Christ priest, in Alhambra, California, February 27, 2004.

[75] Spero Forum, "Baptist, Protestant, and Catholic Discussion—Mel Gibson—'Passion'," www.speroforum.com, February, 23, 2004.

in every nook and cranny of this planet even until this very moment. We do have to watch, and we have to care; and we, if we are to survive it, to have any chance of making sense of it, we better have someone there with whom to share the watching.[76]

"It Is As It Was"

In early December 2003, Steve McEveety, the producer of *The Passion of the Christ* and its assistant director, Jan Michelini, arranged a screening of the film for Pope John Paul II. The pope and his secretary Archbishop Stanislaw Dziwisz were curious to see the movie due to all of the controversy that surrounded it. When the movie ended, the pope is reputed to have commented to his secretary: "It is as it was." These words convey the message that Gibson's portrayal of the death of Jesus was historically truthful. His words endorsed the film. News of the Holy Father's reaction spread all over the world.

However, the Catholic News Service suspected that the pope never made such a comment and was told by a senior Vatican official close to the pope that, indeed, John Paul II did not remark about the movie, as the "Holy Father does not comment, does not give judgments on art."

However, much to his credit, *New York Times* columnist Frank Rich tracked down the story. He spoke in person with Jan Michelini. Michelini confirmed that, after the movie, the pope's secretary convened a meeting in the pope's apartment with him and McEveety and "There, Michelini says, the archbishop quoted the pope not only as saying, 'It is as it was,' but also calling the moving 'incredible.'"[77] It appears very likely that the pope did

---

[76] Sloan.

[77] Frank Rich, "Chutzpah and Spiritual McCarthyism," *The New York Times*, January 16, 2004.

make the statement and he meant it to remain his private opinion.

In any case, "It is as it was," expresses the point of view of millions of viewers all over the world. And indeed, the movie has had an incredible influence literally all over the world. For instance, even though the Chinese government banned the movie because of its religious content, pirated copies of the film played to small gatherings all over the country. Many young agnostics and atheists viewed the film and were provoked to discuss spiritual issues and ask spiritual questions. "A Chinese webmaster who asked to remain anonymous, said the film has created a buzz on Internet discussion forums in China, and 'quite a number of laypeople said they felt their faith strengthened after watching it.'"[78]

The Passion of the Christ has had a great impact in Arab countries. In Saudi Arabia, where expressions of religion other than Islam are banned, *Arab News* reported that "pirated copies of the DVD have been selling like hotcakes on the black market."[79] In Egypt, the Egyptian Censorship Authority relaxed its censorship rules for *The Passion*. Muslims forbid any portrayal of a prophet and Jesus is considered a prophet in Islam. Besides Egypt, *The Passion* was released uncensored in Syria, Lebanon, Jordan, Bahrain, Qatar and the United Arab Emirates.[80] Even Palestinian president Yasir Arafat saw the movie and said it was "historical and impressive."[81] However, many Arabs are interested in the film because they see themselves as persecuted by

---

[78] "Pirated Copies of Gibson Movie Stir Chinese," World Net Daily, www.worldnetdaily.com, April 1, 2004.

[79] "The Passion of the Christ Goes International," World Press Review, www.worldpress.org, May 2004.

[80] Charles Levinson, "Arab Censors Giving 'Passion' Wide Latitude," *Chronicle* foreign service, www.SFGate.com, April 1, 2004.

[81] "President Arafat: Passion of the Christ 'Impressive'," International Press Center, Palestinian National Authority, www.ipc.gov, March 21, 2004.

the Jews, and identify with Jesus as a victim.[82] A Middle Eastern news correspondent wrote, "Mel Gibson's movie *The Passion of the Christ* is moving many Muslims in the Middle East to tears. Long lines form in front of movie theaters in the Jordanian capital Amman.... According to eyewitnesses, Arab audiences are deeply moved by Christ's suffering. Street venders are offering pirated copies. DVDs and videos sell like hot cakes according to the British information service Ekklesia."[83] In Lebanon more than 142,000 people saw *The Passion* on opening day. This broke previous records set by *Titanic* and the James Bond film *Die Another Day*."[84] The movie however, has been virtually banned in Israel. Eli Yishai, leader of the largest political party in Israel said that "showing the movie will give a stage to wicked and deceitful ideas." Moreover, film distributors did not want to take a financial risk on a film that probably would not appeal to a Jewish audience.[85]

Miracles

Very few movies have ever been credited with causing miracles—but one couple believes that *The Passion of the Christ* was at least indirectly responsible for saving their daughter. This miracle was featured in "Changed Lives: Miracles of the Passion," a TV documentary about the Gibson film. A young couple from

---

[82] Levinson. Mustafa Darwish, former president of the Egypt Censorship Authority stated, "They (the censorship authorities) think the film is anti-Semitic. That's why they're giving it such privilege." Mohiy el-Din Abdel Aleem, a professor of media and journalism at Al Azhar University stated, "I encouraged the movie because it withholds from the Jews their claim that they are innocent of Jesus' blood."

[83] Wolfgang Polzer, "'The Passion of the Christ' Moves Arabs," Assist News Service, www.assistnews.net, March 26, 2004.

[84] Levinson.

[85] Joshua Mitnick, "'Passion' Absent from Israeli Theaters," *The Washington Times*, February 27, 2004.

Colorado was interviewed on the program. They told the story of their 11-month-old daughter who drowned in the bathtub. They were absolutely certain their little girl had died. The couple meditated on the scourging of Christ at the pillar as depicted in *The Passion* and prayed "By his stripes we are healed." The parents attribute the full recovery of their daughter to this meditation and prayer.

As this chapter has demonstrated, most of the fruits of *The Passion* are spiritual. The Catholic News Agency reported a story, April 5, 2004, with the headline: "My son died in peace thanks to *The Passion of the Christ.*" Twenty-four year old Ivan Jose Baez lived most of his life embittered about his father who had abandoned him and his mother when he was a small child. His mother raised him in the Catholic faith, but upon adulthood he had left the Church. However Ivan agreed to see *The Passion* with his mother. Within two weeks of seeing the movie Ivan unexpectedly died of a heart attack while riding a bicycle. Ivan had decided to join the Marines and was training for the admission requirements. His heartbroken mother stated that after Ivan's death she found two poetic letters in his room. One was titled "For Mom." In it he thanked his mother for his life. The other letter was called "To the father I never had." In this letter Ivan told his father how much he had suffered because of his father's abandonment of the family. But the letter ended: "Today I say to you, it doesn't matter what you did. I forgive you. I forgive you for hitting my mother. I forgive you for lying to me. I forgive you for forgetting about me, but even more for forgetting about my brothers who were so little when you left us. I forgive you for being the father I needed... and I ask God to forgive you your sins. I still love you and I know you love me."

Ivan's mother was filled with a great peace that her son died with forgiveness in his heart. She states, "Mel Gibson and his movie helped Ivan find Jesus and be able to forgive even those who hurt him most.... God called my son home. It is difficult to understand for any mother and although I suffer for his loss, my heart is at peace. Perhaps for many, *The Passion of the Christ* is just a great movie, but for me it was the instrument that God used to reach my son... it was the instrument God used so my son could go home in peace."

The Passion of the Christ is not just another movie based on the Gospels and the teachings of the Christian religion. It was created by a man of deep, personal religious commitment who *intended* to express the faith of the Church in art. As a work of art, *The Passion* is certainly one of the most controversial, debated, discussed and analyzed movies ever made. However, no matter what controversy and debate the movie has ignited, *The Passion* stands as an authentic *religious* work of art. It ultimately must be evaluated as such. It is religious art because it was made not only to express or represent the Christian faith, but to glorify God. In this sense, it is a kind of icon. It draws the viewer into the Truth and, like a great religious painting—affirming and reminding—it may bring the viewer to an experience of grace.

The Passion and Other Film "Passions"

The Passion of the Christ is the most theologically informed movie ever made about Jesus. As a finely crafted and beautifully filmed movie it is a visual feast, but it is also a theological feast.

This book is not a movie review. While I do have a degree in theater arts and have a lot of knowledge about film and filmmaking, this book does not analyze the artistic merits of *The Passion* as a motion picture. I leave the final verdict on that point to experts in the field of film study. However, I think it is important to examine the spiritual contribution of the Gibson film against other important and influential movies abut Jesus.

Most professional movie critics point to Pier Paolo Pasolini's 1964 film *The Gospel According to Saint Matthew* as the finest film about Jesus ever made. It is well-known that Pasolini, who was murdered on a beach in Ostia, was a committed social revolutionary—a homosexual, Marxist, atheist who had gotten himself into trouble both with civil authorities and the Catholic Church. Many are surprised that such a filmmaker could have turned out such a reverent account of Christ's life as did Pasolini. The film was dedicated to Pope John XXIII. Much of the reverent quality of the movie and its definite sense of respect for Christ and Christianity can be accounted for by the fact that Pasolini's movie is virtually a literal cinematic account of Matthew's Gospel. Indeed, all of the dialogue in the film is taken directly from

Scripture. As one critic stated, people have to almost "know of Pasolini's atheism to see anything unflattering in this portrayal of Jesus."[1]

Critics praise the movie for its grim, gritty, realistic documentary style (in the school of post-war Italian Realism), for the Jesus who appears very human and "desanctified," for Pasolini's casting local amateurs in the film, and for the film's absence of the usual Hollywood grandeur and spectacle that often accompanies Tinseltown's treatment of biblical subjects. Pasolini's depiction of Christ's suffering is not only different from the usual Hollywood versions, but it is also very different from the Gibson film. While Gibson wanted to emphasize the enormity of Christ's sacrifice, watching the Pasolini movie, one gets the impression that this director wanted to de-emphasize Christ's suffering. The Pasolini Jesus doesn't really appear to suffer all that much. While the Passion in *The Passion of the Christ* is drenched in blood, the crucifixion in *The Gospel According to Saint Matthew* is nearly bloodless. Contrary to Matthew's Gospel, there is absolutely no scourging at the pillar. It's not that Jesus, as in *The Greatest Story Ever Told*, is scourged but we don't see it—Jesus is simply not scourged at all. In the Gibson movie all of the action takes place in proximate camera shots. Everything is up-close; nothing is remote or distant. However in the Pasolini movie, for example, Christ's trial before Pilate takes place far, far away over there someplace. Though we can hear the dialogue, we can barely make out the characters. Supposedly this far away shot is meant to make the theater audience part of the crowd in attendance at the trial. However, Pasolini has placed the audience so far away from the action that you feel it is something that is taking place very far from you and that what's happening has nothing to do with you. How different this is from *The Passion of the Christ* in

---

[1] Mary Mapes, "The Gospel According to St. Matthew," Movie Habit, www.moviehabit.com.

which we see and hear everything, all voices, all gestures, all facial expressions that convey anger, doubt, fear and anxiety.

In Pasolini's film Jesus walks the Via Dolorosa almost as if He were taking a stroll, albeit wearing a crown of thorns, but even this torture instrument seems to barely touch Him. It rests like a nest on top of His head. Jesus is even handed some refreshment along the way, which He takes and drinks.

When Jesus gets to Golgotha, one of the thieves shows terrible anguish when he is laid on the cross and nailed to it, but in comparison Jesus is crucified almost silently. There is minimal anguish and minimal blood. The only blood visible on Christ is one small trickle down the right side of the actor's forehead. Mary on the other hand is believably shown in great mourning for her Son. Jesus utters only one loud, dutiful cry from the cross and dies. Immediately upon His death an earthquake erupts. There is a shot of Jesus' burial. Wrapped in a shroud, His feet are visible, but there are no wounds.

Most startling, when Jesus is taken down from the cross (another scene shot from far away) the crown of thorns is thoughtlessly tossed aside. Perhaps Pasolini was making a statement against the Catholic Church's "obsession" with relics. This gesture is absolutely the opposite of the Gibson film. When Jesus is taken down from the cross the very bloody crown of thorns and the nails that pierced His hands and feet are carefully set aside. Instead of being tossed away as so much rubbish, the camera deliberately focuses on them. They have meaning because they point to the sacrifice Christ endured for the salvation of the world and are holy because of that sacrifice.

While *The Passion of the Christ* has been accused of an unfair and negative portrayal of the Jews, *The Gospel According to Saint Matthew* certainly highlights Jesus' conflict with the Sanhedrin. In keeping with the Gospel, the Pharisees are shown as the enemies of Christ throughout the movie. They are shown trying to trip Jesus up, Jesus tells them that the Kingdom of God will be taken from the Jews and given to another people, He calls the Scribes and Pharisees hypocrites, whitened sepulchers, that the Jews will persecute His followers, and Jerusalem will be made desolate. The climax to all these speeches is a view of a dead fig tree, symbol of a Jerusalem that is dead to the message of Christ. It's interesting that the Pasolini movie has not been accused of anti-Semitism.

The Gospel According to Saint Matthew has its controversial aspects. For instance, it displays a subtle, underlying Marxist ideology. However, until *The Passion of the Christ*, the Jesus-related movie that generated the most controversy and debate is Martin Scorsese's 1988 *The Last Temptation of Christ*. Based on the Nikos Kazantzakis novel of the same name, this Jesus is so utterly contrary to the historical Christ of the Gospels, it is fair to say that the confused, tortured-in-soul, and even sinful Jesus of *The Last Temptation* is not Jesus at all. Scorsese tells the viewer in the very beginning that his movie is not based on the Gospels. Not without good reason, many devout Christians find this movie blasphemous.[2] *The Last Temptation of Christ* is what happens to Jesus when atheists, agnostics and skeptics who are very high-minded, serious thinkers, get hold of Him. The film intends to explore the human conflict between spirit and flesh. As one critic observed, Martin Scorsese "is working out of the center of his talents—and his obsessions—as a filmmaker.... Scorsese shows us a Christ who is more an anguished modern neurotic than a biblical figure, a sort of Hamlet, and seemingly unfit for his role as Messiah. And he invites us to think of him as mad."[3]

The vast difference between the Scorsese Jesus and the Gibson Jesus results from the fact that Scorsese is alienated from Christianity and Catholicism, while these are the center of

---

[2] For a full critique of this issue see: Steven D. Greydanus, "*The Last Temptation of Christ*: An Essay in Film Criticism and Faith," www.decentfilms.com, 2001.

[3] Hal Hinson, "The Last Temptation of Christ," *Washington Post*, August 12, 1988.

Gibson's life. In *The Last Temptation* we have a Jesus for atheists repugnant to most committed believers. In *The Passion* we have a Jesus for believers repugnant to committed unbelievers. The Jesus of *The Last Temptation*, while he may illustrate the human dilemma, cannot claim in any way to be the true Son of God.

However the Scorsese and the Gibson movie do have some similarities. The music, for example, is amazingly similar and makes one wonder if the composers dipped into the same Middle-Eastern musical sources. In each film the Devil is real and, in each film, tries to derail the accomplishment of Christ's mission. *The Passion of the Christ* affirms the Real Presence and the sacrificial nature of the Eucharist. *The Last Temptation*, in a weird and macabre kind of way, also makes a statement that the Eucharist is the true Body and Blood of Christ. At the Last Supper Peter drinks from the cup. He then puts his fingers in his mouth and blood trickles from his mouth and pools in his hand. It's clear that this beverage is not just wine, but Christ's blood.

Like *The Passion*, *The Last Temptation* has a shocking scourging and crucifixion if for no other reason than that Christ is depicted as naked. If believers can identify with Jesus in this movie, the naked body of the Lord can stimulate spiritual awareness of the terrible humiliation Christ endured. Like *The Passion* the camera focuses on the nail driven through Jesus' hand with the point protruding through the back of the cross. And also, like *The Passion* Mary and Mary Magdalen kneel when Christ is on the cross. Like *The Passion*, some viewers found *The Last Temptation* very violent and bloody:

> The film is awash in blood; it is the ruling visual motif. (Even the opening credits are cast against a blood-red backing, and under them we hear Peter Gabriel's pulsing music.) But then again, blood is its subject— blood and fire and the frailties of the flesh.[4]

---

4   Hinson.

However, compared to *The Passion of the Christ*, *The Last Temptation* is hardly "awash in blood." If this reviewer thinks blood in the Scorsese film is the "ruling visual motif" one could easily say to him "You ain't seen nothing yet!"

While both movies are focused on religious themes and issues, the differences between the two movies are vast. I will mention two of the most important differences.

The first difference has to do with each filmmaker's approach to religion in general. Perhaps the biggest offense committed by both Kazantzakis and Scorsese is their willingness to take advantage of and exploit the Christian religion, its sacred symbols, beliefs, and Scriptures to work out their own private philosophical questions and conflicts. They are artists who gave up the Christian faith, but who use the Christian religion, a religion that others hold sacred, to publicly work out and articulate their own doubts. One can at least seriously raise the question whether anyone, including artists, have the moral right to pervert religious symbols for their own private artistic expression. In any case, whether they have that right or not, that is what Scorsese did in *The Last Temptation*. Gibson, on the contrary, set out to make a movie, while certainly a personal expression of his religious commitment, that deliberately honors and respects the meaning of the Christian religion—and in this sense it is not his *private* expression. *The Passion* reflects the Christian religion, indeed the faith of the Church. *The Last Temptation* is the kind of movie that uses the Christian religion, even perverts it, for the sake of exploration of personal philosophical and spiritual issues.

This second difference is the *result* of the two filmmakers' attitude towards Christianity. In *The Last Temptation* Jesus, even when he is already on the cross, wavers in his mission. He is not really, completely on the cross yet. His commitment to the redemptive mission is undecided, confused and insecure, even unreliable, as is his willingness to take on the duties of the Messiah. The Christ of the Gibson movie, once He has surrendered to the Father's will in the opening scene, is a Christ filled with a resolute spirit. He is a committed Jesus. He enters the Passion with His whole self, and literally, nothing of soul or body is withheld. While the Christ of *The Last Temptation* reflects ambivalence towards the redemption of man, the Christ of *The Passion* is a sure Savior, someone we can count on. The fate of the human race is not a "maybe" in His hands. The ambivalent Christ of the Scorsese film reflects the director's own stance towards God. The sure Christ of *The Passion* reflects Gibson's Lord and is the Christ of faith. It is interesting to note that in the Gibson film and the Scorsese film, Jesus is kissed while on the cross. In *The Last Temptation* Satan kisses Jesus—in the guise of a little girl who leads him away from his mission. In *The Passion* Jesus is kissed by His mother who desires to die with Him, who throughout the film has affirmed Christ in the accomplishment of His salvific mission.

Perhaps the best Hollywood Jesus movie, since Cecil B. DeMille's 1927 silent *The King of Kings* is the 1961 remake entitled *King of Kings* starring the very handsome Jeffrey Hunter as Christ. Hunter plays the part of the Savior with warmth, dignity and restraint. Some critics made fun of the movie because of Hunter's youngish looks and dubbed it *I Was A Teenage Jesus*, as a joking reference to such movies as *I Was A Teenage Werewolf*, and because the movie was directed by Nicholas Ray, who also directed the classic James Dean film *Rebel Without a Cause*. However, the harsher criticisms of the movie are unfair. It is a decent presentation of the life of Christ and is generally well-acted and contains a very stirring and majestic musical score by Miklos Rozsa.

Theologically, however, the movie is not deep. It intends to present a pretty straightforward story about the life of Christ with reverence and awe for the subject matter. Jesus is without question Christ the Son of God. It is, as a Hollywood picture, big-scale and lavish. Similar to *The Passion*, Jesus has a very close relationship with His mother and she is presented as completely in tune with her Son's identity and mission and even accompanies Him to Jerusalem. Also similar to *The Passion*, King Herod is totally corrupt and is even presented as a sexual pervert—as he lusts for his stepdaughter Salome. The 1976 Franco Zeffirelli film *Jesus of Nazareth* also depicted King Herod as sexually attracted to his stepdaughter. In *The Passion* it is implied that Herod is perhaps either homosexual or bi-sexual. In any case, it seems the character of Herod is often portrayed in film as sexually perverse. It is interesting to compare the scene where Jesus is taken to Herod in the 1965 George Stevens film *The Greatest Story Ever Told* to the same scene in *The Passion*. In both films Herod is enjoying himself in a debauched party atmosphere that is interrupted by the serious and rejected Jesus. While Herod in the Gibson film is very effeminate, Herod in the Stevens movie, played by José Ferrer, appears at least mildly effeminate.

One extreme difference between *King of Kings* and *The Passion* is their depiction of the Jewish leaders. In *King of Kings* Caiaphas is given a practical reason for seeking the death of Jesus. He proclaims that Jesus is a threat and that Pilate will use Jesus as an excuse to crush the Jews. The audience is presented with a political reason why the Jewish leaders want Jesus to be killed. There is no trial before the Sanhedrin at all. We only know that such a trial took place when dialogue is given to Pilate that informs us about it. Moreover, there is no crowd scene in front of Pilate either. The audience learns about this when the Roman centurion enters the prison cell of Barabbas, unlocks his chains and tells him that the people preferred him to Jesus who has been condemned to die. It is interesting how *King of Kings* stays clear of involving the Jewish leaders in the death of Christ. It is simply not dramatized.

Like *The Passion*, Mary and John accompany Jesus on the Via Dolorosa. The walk to Calvary is very quiet and the film is preoccupied with Judas's reaction to it. The scourging of Christ at the pillar is shown very briefly, but nearly all the details of the crucifixion of Christ are not shown. The audience hears the nails being driven into Christ's hands, but it is not shown. The cross is raised up—a scene shot from above the cross. Mary, as in *The Passion*, kneels at Calvary.

A sure sign that *King of Kings* wants to stay clear of any profound theologizing is seen in the way Jesus addresses Mary. The words from the Gospel of John are edited. Jesus looks at His mother and says to her, "Behold your son." It is very obvious that the words indicate Him, not John. John is not standing anywhere within the movie frame and Jesus doesn't say to him, "Son, behold your mother." There's no attempt at a New Eve, Mary Mother of the Church, or Mary as the proto-Christian here. Mary, while a very special and holy woman, is just Jesus' mom.

Perhaps the one thing *King of Kings* and *The Passion of the Christ* share is the fact that both films intend for Jesus to be very visible, very proximate and, while certainly the divine Son of God, also very real. After DeMille's *The King of Kings* in 1927 the character of Jesus went into hiding. I mean, of course, that nearly every movie up until 1961 did not dare show the face of Jesus. The divine and holy Son of God is a mystery and filmmakers respected that mystery by not showing the audience Jesus' face. Jesus is after all God Himself, the One, True, Universal God. This mystery is "spoilt" if this God suddenly appears with a particular face. Particularity seems to reduce His majesty and divinity. The movies *The Robe* (1953) and *Ben Hur* (1959) present us with good examples of the "invisible" Jesus. The actors depicting Christ in such movies are very artfully filmed from behind, or from above, or the camera will focus on just a hand or foot. The scenes in which Jesus appears are, nonetheless, quite effective and moving, but a cinematic barrier has been erected between the audience and Jesus. He remains apart from us. We can never really enter His space. Much was made of the fact that in the 1961 *King of Kings*, Jesus was (for the first time in decades) fully presented. The trailer of the movie emphasized this point with the dramatic voiceover stating, "In *King of Kings* you will behold the figure of Jesus Christ in a living characterization." This is why it was probably very important for the makers of this movie to present a Jesus that looked like everyone's idea of Him—engaging, handsome, blue-eyed, serious, dignified, idealized and maybe even deliberately ethnically European—as opposed to a Middle-Eastern Jew.

Like *King of Kings* Gibson's Jesus is a real particular man whose face is open to the audience, and the presentation of Jesus is thus vulnerable to audience acceptance or rejection. Jeffrey Hunter's idealized looks helps the Jesus of *King of Kings* to be accepted in His particularity—especially when that particularity has been hidden for so long. Nonetheless, presenting the face of Christ to the judgment of the audience affirms the incarnational truth of the Christian religion. When God became man, He had a *particular* face; a real body and a real face uniquely His own.

Besides *King of Kings*, Hollywood in the decade of the sixties produced another biblical epic, this time based on the popular Fulton Oursler book, *The Greatest Story Ever Told*. The 1965 film, directed by George Stevens, was nearly universally panned by the critics. It is a very slow and boring movie with a slow and boring Jesus played by a reverent but energy-less Max von Sydow. It has been called the *It's a Mad, Mad, Mad, Mad World* of biblical movies due to its being studded, like the comic masterpiece, with all sorts of Hollywood stars. And without intending to be comic, many critics saw the Stevens film that way. Despite its flaws *The Greatest Story* is well-filmed, very pretty to look at, and does have a theological perspective that Christ is the Redeemer who came not just to save the poor and downtrodden, as in the Pasolini movie, but to save all the world from sin, injustice, corruption and death. The director seemed more intent on creating large panoramic views than engaging us with the person of Christ. Almost the entire crucifixion, for instance, is filmed from far away. It's something that takes place in the distance. There are only two close up shots during the entire crucifixion episode. Sydow is crucified without screams or any sign of agony. He is calm, resolute and stoic. Similar to the Gibson film, we do see, though briefly, the nail positioned into the palm of Christ's left hand, but the actual nailing is done off screen. It must be remembered that this is the 1960s, way before the censorship code was dropped and film ratings for violence were initiated. Hollywood filmmakers were still sensitive about depicting graphic violence on screen. Christ's walk to Calvary is silent—even peaceful—accompanied by very sad and lyrical music. Simon is conscripted to carry Jesus' cross and, like the Gibson movie, Simon (played by Sidney Poitier) and Jesus carry the cross together. And, like the Gibson movie, the Simon of *The Greatest Story* has to be pushed away from Christ once the summit of Golgotha has been reached.

The high priest, played by Martin Landau, seeks Jesus' death in a rather perfunctory fashion. For most of the movie Caiaphas's interest in Jesus seems aloof, even detached. Not until near the end of Christ's trial before the Sanhedrin do we see any fire in this character. And indeed, the primary blame for the death of Jesus falls to Pontius Pilate. This is conveyed by the character, played by Telly Savalas, as he recites the words of the Apostles Creed, "Suffered under Pontius Pilate," when Jesus is taken away to die. The movie has no scourging scene at all but, when Jesus carries His cross, it is obvious that a scourging did, however, take place.

The Jesus film that attracted great attention and, since its 1976 TV premier has been seen by millions of viewers, is Franco Zeffirelli's very ambitious three-part drama *Jesus of Nazareth*. It is a beautifully mounted production, for the most part faithful to Scripture and even theologically informed. That Zeffirelli consulted Catholic and Protestant scholars is evident in the film. For example, when Jesus cries, "My God, my God why have you forsaken me?" in Aramaic one of the chief priests is astonished that even from the cross Jesus quotes Scripture. In this way the audience is informed that Jesus isn't just proclaiming that He feels abandoned by the Father, but that He is indeed quoting the first line of Psalm 22. The movie has its own theological perspective. The actor Robert Powell plays Jesus with great elegance and shows Him as an authoritative teacher who is very sure of His identity and mission. And Zeffirelli is intent on making Jesus very real, very believable as a human being, but he never departs from presenting Him as the Son of God. The divine nature of Jesus is emphasized by the fact that this character in the film is the only one who has blue eyes—and they are very piercing blue eyes. This signals that Jesus is not completely like the rest of the human race—He's different, He's set apart.

Christ's Passion in the Zeffirelli movie, from the agony in the garden to His last breath on the cross, is a film depiction of Christ's suffering that can compare to *The Passion of the Christ*. It is filmed with deep emotion and intensity and is extremely moving. Christ's walk to Calvary, carrying the cross beam across His shoulders, is filmed like a documentary, the path filled with chaos, angry shouting, some people cursing Christ, tear-filled men and women, people in anguish, and Roman guards intent on accomplishing their task.

The crucifixion scene in *Jesus of Nazareth* is very different from *The Passion of the Christ*, though very effective in recreating a sense of historical authenticity of this Roman torture method. While Gibson dwells on every detail of Christ's execution, the nailing of Jesus to the cross in *Jesus of Nazareth* happens with horrific efficiency. The Roman soldiers have obviously done this dozens of times and Jesus is hung on the cross with cold speed. When Christ reaches the summit of Calvary He is not even permitted to catch His breath and neither is the viewer.

While Zeffirelli's crucifixion scene lacks the slow, graphic horror of the Gibson film, it is a very legitimate and moving interpretation of Christ's suffering.

In the year 2004 another Jesus movie besides *The Passion of the Christ* was released, namely, *The Gospel According to John*. But unlike *The Passion*, audience response to it was lukewarm and minimal. The movie is literally a word for word screen adaptation of the fourth Gospel—including not only the dialogue of the Gospel, but every word of the narrative as it appears in the *Good News Bible* translation of the American Bible Society. It is a dignified, reverent film. However, as a cinematic work of art it lacks creativity. It is also, incredible as this may sound, very short on theology too. It is not enough to put the words of the Bible up on the screen. Each Gospel has particular theological issues and themes that are central to it. John, for instance, takes the Incarnation of God very seriously. It is based on theological categories of light versus darkness, life versus death, this world of sin versus the Kingdom of God. None of this theology is cinematically illustrated in the movie. Perhaps the director did not wish to be cinematically creative for fear that more visually provocative and stimulating images would overpower and distract from the verbal Gospel text.

However, other, non-literal theological ideas are presented in the movie. Most notably, for example, Mary Magdalen is always hanging out with The Twelve as if she were indeed the thirteenth apostle. She is even blessed by Jesus as He blesses the apostles when He speaks about the meaning of discipleship in His final discourse. The film was advertised as a literal word for word depiction of John's Gospel, but such a scene is not in the Gospel. But, technically speaking, the movie was still a word for word presentation. Perhaps Peter Saville, the movie's director, used the film as an opportunity to make his own statement on the rights of women.

However, similar to the Gibson film, *The Gospel According*

167

to John definitely shows the chief priests calling for Christ's death and also shows Pontius Pilate conflicted and in distress over his role in that death. It is interesting however to note that *The Gospel According to John* movie changes words that appear in the New Testament text. Throughout the fourth Gospel, those who oppose Christ and reject Him are called "the Jews." For John "the Jews" is a theological category—a sign of the world that does not know Christ. However, whenever the Johannine term, "the Jews" is used in his Gospel, the movie, perhaps understandably sensitive to anti-Semitism, changed the words to "the Jewish leaders."

It is ironic that *The Passion of the Christ*—so filled with extra biblical language and gestures—compared to *The Gospel According to John* that stuck completely to the words of the New Testament, is the more theologically complex and profound film.

Perhaps the one Jesus movie that can really compare to the importance of *The Passion* is the Cecil B. DeMille 1927 silent version of *The King of Kings*. Like *The Passion*, *The King of Kings* ignited fears of anti-Semitism which never materialized. Even DeMille lamented, "In spite of excellent reviews... what was harder to comprehend and cope with was the organized opposition of certain Jewish groups to the filmed history of the greatest Jew who ever lived." Joseph Farah of World Net Daily, an Internet Catholic news service, commented on the impact of the silent *The King of Kings* in comparison to *The Passion*. Evidence of the silent movie's impact is that thirty-two years after its release over 800 million people all over the world had seen it. Because it was a silent movie, missionaries used it to teach the Christian religion in non-English-speaking countries. *The Passion of the Christ*, a movie in two dead languages, also has this potential. Another similarity between the two movies is the attitude of the filmmakers toward the subject matter. DeMille was very aware that he was dealing with a sacred subject and demanded that his cast and crew swear off immoral living while the movie was being filmed. This was especially difficult for alcoholic H.B. Warner who played Jesus. The movie was in production for a year. As soon as it was over, however, the poor actor went back to his drinking habits.

The silent *The King of Kings* is most like *The Passion* in the way this movie influenced 1920's audiences. The film converted many people. One of the most famous conversions was H.E. Wallner, who saw the movie in Germany prior to World War II. He became a Christian and in 1939 was the pastor of a church in Prague when Adolf Hitler invaded Czechoslovakia. One of his parishioners, a Jewish doctor who had converted to Christianity, was sent to a concentration camp. The doctor was so severely beaten and abused that he had to have an arm amputated.

One night a Nazi officer banged the doctor's head against a wall. Blood poured down his face and, according to DeMille, the officer mocked him saying, "Take a look at yourself. Now you look like your Jewish Christ." The man responded, "Lord, never in my life have I received such an honor—to resemble You." The doctor died from his wounds.

The officer was exceedingly disturbed by what he had done and sought help in a nearby church. It happened to be Wallner's church. The pastor prayed with him and told him, "Perhaps God let you kill that good man to bring you to the foot of the cross, where you can help others." The German officer, with Wallner and the Czech underground aided hundreds of Jews who would have wound up in similar camps. In 1957 Wallner told Cecil B. DeMille, "If it had not been for *The King of Kings*, I would not be a Lutheran pastor, and 350 Jewish children would have died in the ditches."

Any movie about Jesus has the potential to be a great film, because the subject matter of the Christian faith deals with the most significant dimensions of human life. The Judeo/Christian religion is eminently filmable because, unlike any other religion, the order of this world is taken seriously. History is the arena of

God's activity and with the advent of Judaism, history becomes a real category. Our world is the world of God's action and man's response. The Judeo/Christian faith is a faith based on real historical events that matter. These events are filled with high drama. Certainly, from a theological, if not historical point of view, the drama of God's entry into the world of time is the highest drama. But this God is not a ghost—He has flesh, He has blood, He has a face and a voice, hands that touch others, feet that literally trod the earth. Because the Lord deemed to be one of us, His divine image can be "caught." He has allowed Himself to be caught by us. The history of movies about Jesus is a history of trying to catch the Lord. In the history of film *The Passion of the Christ* catches Him in a new and unique way. Gibson may have caught Him, the God of history, but in the net of the cinematic screen—in the net of the living incarnational image of the Lord's suffering love—He catches us.

ST PAULS

This book was produced by St. Pauls/Alba House, the Society of St. Paul, an international religious congregation of priests and brothers dedicated to serving the Church through the communications media.

For information regarding this and associated ministries of the Pauline Family of Congregations, write to the Vocation Director, Society of St. Paul, P.O. Box 189, 9531 Akron-Canfield Road, Canfield, Ohio 44406-0189. Phone (330) 702-0359; or E-mail: spvocationoffice@aol.com or check our internet site, www.albahouse.org